THE ART AND SCIENCE
OF
PERSONAL MAGNETISM

THE ART AND SCIENCE OF
PERSONAL MAGNETISM

THERON Q. DUMONT

COSIMO CLASSICS
NEW YORK

Cosimo, P.O. Box 416
Old Chelsea Station
New York, NY 10113-0416

or visit our website at:
www.cosimobooks.com

The Art and Science of Personal Magnetism originally published by the
Yogi Publications Society in 1913.

Library of Congress Cataloging-in-Publication Data
A catalog record for this book is available from the Library of Congress

Cover design by www.wiselephant.com

ISBN: 1-59605-349-6

CONTENTS

PRELIMINARY GREETING.

I take pleasure in presenting to the many American students who will acquire possession of copies of this book, these practical lessons on the Art and Science of Personal Magnetism These chapters contain the gist of the lessons taught by me, in classes, and to individuals, in my courses of personal instruction conducted by me, here in Paris, for the past eighteen years. In my personal class work, of course, I adapt the instruction to the special requirements of my individual students, which I cannot do in the case of general lessons in printed form. But, notwithstanding this, I feel that I have condensed into these pages the essence of my methods, and principles of practice, so that any student of average intelligence may readily grasp, assimilate, and apply the same with success. At least, I feel that if the student does not accomplish this, it will be his or her own fault, not that of myself.

In introducing this book, I wish to express my obligations to Mr. L. N. D., an American student of mine, here in Paris, who has kindly transformed my rather stilted "guide book

English" into the plain, simple form desirable for a book designed for the general public. I feel particularly indebted to him for supplying the idiomatic, American "man on the street" terms, thus reproducing the conversational style which I use in all my lessons in French, but which my "book English" rendered impossible in this case without the kindly assistance of this worthy gentleman.

With hand on heart, I send to my new American audience the snicere regards, and most earnest wishes for success, of

Their solicitous teacher,

THERON Q. DUMONT

Paris, France.

CHAPTER I.

PERSONAL MAGNETISM.

It is a strange and almost amusing fact that there should be at the same time, on the part of the general public, such a general acceptance of the existence of personal magnestism, on the one hand, and such an ignorance of the nature of this wonderful force, on the other hand. In short, while everyone believes in the existence of personal magnetism, scarcely anyone possesses a knowledge of the real nature of the same, much less a working knowledge of its principles of application.

A belief in the existence of a personal power, influence, or atmosphere, on the part of certain individuals, which enables the possessor to attract, influence, dominate or control others, has been held by the race from the earliest days of written history. Many of the oldest writings of the race contain references to the strange, mysterious power possessed by certain individuals, which enabled them to attract or influence others. And, following the course of written human history along the ages, we may perceive a constant reference to this strange power of the individual, so generaly acknowledged and, at the same time, so little understood.

Coming down to the present age, an age in which great attention has been devoted to the study of psychology and psychic subjects in general, we find that while the old belief in personal magnetism has been strengthened, there exists, at the same time, very little general knowledge among the public regarding the real nature of the force or the best means of using and employing it.

But this lack of knowledge just alluded to is confined to the general public. In all ages there have been a few advanced individuals who have thoroughly understood and employed the force of personal influence. Not only have the occult students of the past possessed this knowledge, and have passed it on to their successors, but many of the greatest men of history have acquired a thorough knowledge likewise, and have employed it in advancing their own interests. In some cases, individuals of this last mentioned class have received direct instruction from occult teachers, but in many cases they have stumbled across the existence of the power within themselves, and then advanced in their knowledge of the subject by careful investigation and study, accompanied by constant experimentation. Many of them, in their writings or sayings, have testified to their knowledge and use of this most wonderful power.

It is difficult even to correctly define the term "personal magnetism," so little are its principles understood by the masses of the people. The dictionaries give us but little help in the matter, so vague are their so-called definitions. Perhaps the best definition is the following: "The strong, peculiar, but little understood power, force, or influence, exerted by certain individuals, in varying degrees, by the means of which other persons are attracted to, controlled by, dominated, or influenced by the individual possessing the power; a form of mental influence exerted by certain individuals over those with whom they come in contact."

The principal objection that I, personally, have to the above otherwise fairly good definition, is it implies that personal magnetism is possessed by only certain individuals, the implication being that the remainder of the race are devoid of it. This, in my opinion, is a sad mistake. The truth is that each and every individual is possessed of a certain degree of personal magnetism, and that each person may increase the degree and strengthen the power, by knowledge and practice. Even the most "unmagnetic" person possesses personal magnetism, perhaps even to a consderable degree, but is generally so ignorant of the nature of the force or the means of its employment, that he or she actually repels other persons instead of attractnig them. For, do not fail to note this fact, personal magnetism, like material magnetism, may repel as well as attract—it has its positive as well as its negative side. Many very repelent persons are really manifesting a high degree of personal magnetism, in a negative form, and are driving away persons from them in the same manner that others attract persons to them—it is all a matter of the use of the power.

The fact is that every person generates and throws off a certain degree (varying among different individuals) of personal magnetism, which affects the minds of other persons coming within the field of its influence. Not noly does each person emanate and project a certain amount or degree of personal magnetism, but each person also is constantly surrounded by a field of personal magnetic influence—a personal atmosphere, so to speak. This personal atmosphere affects to a greater or less degree other persons coming within its field of influence.

This personal atmosphere varies greatly in degree of strength, extent and general character, among different individuals. The average person has but a weak personal atmosphere, which extends but a short distance on all sides of him, while the strong characters of the race are surrounded by a widely spread personal atmosphere of great power, especially when they are aroused by any strong emotion, feeling or desire. The personal atmosphere of those strong individuals, who are generally recognized as leaders of the race, usually extends great distances from the person, and is fairly saturated with strong dynamic magnetism which impresses itself strongly upon those coming within their field of influence.

But even the weaker individuals of the race, are using personal magnetism unconsciously, exert at least some degree of influence upon those around them. It requires but a moment's thought to recognize that some persons emanate an atmosphere of good-cheer, brightness, and happiness, which affects in a desirable way all persons with whom they come in contact. Others, in the same way, are surrounded by an atmopshere of gloom, pessimism and discouragement, which adversely affects persons coming near them. These things are too common to even excite interest among the average persons, but in this phenomena may be found the key to the higher forms of personal magnetism.

We are so accustomed to regarding personal magnetism as meaning only the positive, attractive phase, that it comes as a shocks to some of us to be told that the repelling personal atmosphere is equally "magnetic"—that is, magnetic in the wrong direction. This should cause no wonder, when we remember that even the physical metallic magnet repels, under some circumstances, as strongly as it attracts under others. There are, it is true, certain individuals who seem neither to attract or repel, but this does not affect the general rule. These neutral individuals are usually of weak magnetism, and weak character—that is to say they have no very strong motives, aims or desires, or strong cast of character or personality. Each faculty of the mentality is neutralized by some other faculty of equal strength, and the result is a neutral condition akin to luke-warm water—neither hot nor cold. It follows, naturally, that such persons exert but a neutral influence, and have but a weak neutral personal atmosphere. They neither attract nor repel—they simply "bore" persons with whom they come in contact.

Some may raise the question that if, as I have said, each and every person is possessed of personal magnetism, then why should any one bother any more about the matter, or study the subject of personal magnetism at all. Such a question (and it is frequently raised, for that matter) causes a smile to manifest on the features of those who have a knowledge of the subject, so childish does it seem to them. While it is true that each and every person is possessed of personal magnetism to some degree, it is equally true that the majority of persons have but a weak magnetic force, and that often of a negative or undesirable character. And, it is a fact positively known to those who have mastered the subject, that even the weakest and most negative person may so develop his or her personal magnetism as to gradually acquire the same degree and character of magnetism as that possessed by many individuals originally far in advance of them in magnetic influence.

One may completely change the character of his personal magnetism, from negative to positive, from undesirable to desirable, by careful study and practice along the lines which I shall lay down in this book. Moreover, it is possible for any person possessing sufficient will, perserverance and determination, to develop from a puny state of magnetism into a condition of giant magnetic powers. But this latter requires determination, constant practice until a certain stage is reached, and an indomitable will. While any one may easily increase his or her degree of power of personal magnetism, and still more easily change the character of one's personal atmosphere, the higher prizes are reserved for those who will persevere to the end, and continue faithful in the exercises. This, of course, is true not only of personal magnetism, but also of every other thing worth having. There is no royal road to anything worth having. We must work for what we get. The prizes are not for the weaklings and triflers, but for the persistent, earnest individuals who will "hang on" until. they succeed.

In this little book, I give you the key to the secret of personal magnetism, but it will still remain for you, yourselves, to determine just what degree of success you shall attain. I give you the best tools, and instruction as to how to use them—but you will have to do the rest yourself. This I will say, however, success must and will be yours if you will, following the instructions, carefully, persistently and perseveringly. That is all I can do for you—the rest is in your own hands.

CHAPTER II.

MENTAL AND PHYSICAL POLES.

Some of the writers on the subject of personal magnetism have fallen into the error of considering that the entire secret of personal magnetism is to be found in the phenomena of telepathy or transference of thought. These writers, however, have been so carried away by the wonderful facts of the mental phase of personal magnetism, that they have entirely overlooked the other phase, i. e., the physical pole of the magnetic personality. This second phase is just as important as is the mental phase, and the person who wishes to cultivate and develop personal magnetism must give this second phase the same careful attention and practice as the first phase. There are two distinct phases or poles of personal magnetism, (1) the mental; and (2) the physical. Do not fail to note this fact, for your success will depend upon the coordination of the force of both poles.

To many, this idea of there being a second or physical phase of personal magnetism will seem strange, so accustomed have they grown to hearing the teaching that personal magnetism is a mental phenomenon pure and simple But as we proceed in our study of the subject in this book, I hope to thoroughly convince you that this second pole of personal magnetism really exists, and that it is equally potent with the first, or mental, phase or pole. As man is a dual-organism, with both mental and physical phases of manifestation, both mind and body, so is his personal force composed of two distinct phases or poles, each coordinating energy and creating effects. Some persons with the other in the work of manifesting have more mental magnetism, while others have more physical magnetism, but the individual who really manifests the highest degree of perosnal magnetism is the one who is developed along both poles of activity, both phases of magnetism—physical as well as mental.

The mental pole or phase of personal magnetism depends for its force and energy upon the ability of the mind to create thought-waves and to project them beyond the limits of the brain, into the personal atmosphere of the individual, and even beyond the range of his own personal atmosphere when necessary. When accompanied with the physical magnetism generated by the other pole of magnetic activity, this mental magnetism strongly affects other persons coming within the field of action of these thought-waves. But without a good supply of the physical magnetism, these thought-waves fail to have sufficient strength to produce marked results. It would seem that the physical magnetism were needed to give "body" to the mental magnetism, just as the mental magnetism is needed to give color, character or "soul" to the physical magnetism. The two phases of magnetism must work together to gain the best effects.

It was formerly very difficult to convey to the mind of the student the facts regarding the mental phase of personal magnetism, so strange did the whole thing appear to him. But in these days, when there has been so much written and taught regarding telepathy, thought-transference and mind-power, the average person is so well posted on the general subject that he may readily understand the special features of thought-power as manifested in personal magnetism. So it is not necessary, now, to give the student a thorough education regarding the general subject of telepathy, in order to lead him up to the special subject of personal magnetism. In this book, I shall take it for granted that the student knows something of the subject of telepathy or thought-transference, and accordingly I shall not take up space and time in travelling over this old familiar ground. But, nevertheless, I think it advisable to point out to you some of the latest facts discovered by science in connection with the transference of thought.

Science has dicovered that the human brain, in the process of thinking, actually generates and uses up a certain amount of energy in the area of the brain tissue. The generation and employment of this energy produces heat, and actually increases the temperature of the brain areas, as may be proven by the use of the delicate registering instruments found in every well-equipped laboratory of the day. This energy of the brain is as much an actual force as is electricity or the ordinary magnetism of the lode-stone, and is governed by much the same general laws and rules And, like electricity or ordinary magnetism, it is not confined to the point at which it is generated, but, instead, it may be, and is, diffused to points beyond. In other words, the thought energy of the brain of a person extends beyond the limits of his brain, creates a thought-atmosphere around him, and registers an effect upon the brains of others coming within his field of energy.

The discovery of radio-activity in certain newly discovered elements of matter, notably in the case of radium, has led science to investigate the matter of the possible radio-activity of other substances. The result is most surprising, for advanced science now announces that every substance is radio-active, that is, every substance is constantly radiating energy of force from itself. This discovery serves to harmonize the previously separated facts regarding thought-transference, etc., and it is now accepted as a fact that the human brain is strongly radio-active, and is constantly sending forth streams of thought-energy, just as the bit of radium is constantly sending forth streams of radio-energy. The same laws which govern the radium, are now perceived to govern the brain action. This simplifies the matter, and brings the subject of thought-transference into the general field of science, **and out** of the realms of mysticism. The subject **is** now taught and studied, on a scientific basis, in the principal universities of the world, and new discoveries are constantly being made regarding it.

The physical pole of personal magnetism is not to be found in the flesh, blood, or bones of the body—for these are but the crude machinery by which the higher parts of the human organism moves and acts. Instead, it is to be found in that most wonderful part, or parts, of the organism, known as the **nervous** system. This nervous system is just as wonderful in its way as is the brain, and its effects in personal magnetism are just as important.

We are so apt to think of the nerves as being a part of the "body" of the person, that it is somewhat difficult for us to get the idea that the nervous system is really as much a part of the mental system as is the brain. In fact, the nervous system is composed of almost exactly the same kind of matter as is the brain. The nervous system, moreover, generates energy of a kind very similar to that generated by the brain. For that matter, advanced **science** really considers that the brain **and** nervous system are but parts of one and the same thing, governed by the same general laws, and to be considered in connection with each other. And, the student of personal magnetism soon comes to accept this view, when he sees the important part played by the great nerve centres in the work of personal magnetism. Therefore, although I call the magnetism of the nervous system by the term "physical," and that of the brain by the term "phytal," I do so merely in order to make an easy line of distinction for the purpose of teaching and study. At the last, however, they are really but parts of one and the same thing—merely two poles of the same source of energy.

The nervous system of the human being is really a most intricate mechanism. Its main feature is the spinal cord which runs along an opening in the spinal column or backbone, and which is directly connected with the brain matter in the skull. From the spinal cord emerge many sets of nerves, in pairs, which branch out in smaller filmaments, these in turn branching out into still smaller, and so on, until each and every part of the body is supplied with a direct connection with the main nerve trunk. Other great cables of nerves descend into the trunk of the body, apart from the spinal cord system, although connected with the latter by nerve links. In different parts of the body are to be found great masses of nerve-substance, being matted knots or tangles of nerves, these centres being called plexi or plexuses, the principal one being the "solar plexus" which is situated right back of the pit of the stomach, and which plays a very important part in the life of the person, so important, indeed, that a severe blow struck directly over it may cause the death of the perosn.

The nervous system not only convey messages from the different parts of the body to the brain, but also serves to convey the energy of motion to the various parts. In short, there can be no motion of any part of the nerves. When the nerves governing any part of the body are paralyzed, that part of the body becomes devoid of motion. So you see, the nervous system is a part of the great energy-producing-system of the body—as such a part of it as the brain. Remember this, always, for it is one of the keys to the secrets of personal magnetism.

When you remember that this nerve-energy spreads itself beyond the limits of the body,

just as does the energy of the brain, then you
may begin to see what I am "driving at" in
announcing the second pole or phase of personal magnetism, namely the "physical" pole,
which in realtiy, is the phase of magnetism
generated and radiated by the nervous system, particularly by its great centres of plexi.
I think that you are now beginning to get the
idea, although I have carefully avoid technical,
scientific terms and have expressed myself in
the simplest form.

CAPTER III.

THE MENTAL PHASE.

The mental phase of personal magnetism depends upon two coordinated manifestations of mental power, as follows: (1) the holding of certain mental states until the mental atmosphere becomes charged with the vibrations of the particular mental states; and (2) the conscious projection of the mental current from the brain centres by the action of the will of the individual. I shall now proceed to describe these two mental phases of manifestation in detail.

It is a fact known to all students of the subject that the character of the mental atmosphere of any individual depends entirely upon the character of the mental states held by him. The mental atmosphere of the hopeful, expectant individual is composed of vibrations of a hopeful, cheerful character, which tend to impress and affect other persons coming within the field of activity of his personal atmosphere. Likewise, the mental atmosphere of the gloomy, depressed individual, is composed of vibrations of a gloomy, depressing character, which impresses and affects individuals coming in contact therewith. And, in the same manner, all of one's mental states will become manifest in his mental atmosphere, and accordingly, will affect those with whom he comes in close contact.

The truth of the above statements will become apparent to anyone who will give the matter a moment's careful consderation, remembering at the same time the impressions created upon himself when he has come in contact with different individuals. He will remember that some individuals have left upon him the impression of gloom, inefficiency, failure, etc. Others have left with him a feeling of suspicion, distrust, and uneasiness. Others still have given him the impression of cheerfulness, friendliness, confidence, and good-will.

The atmosphere of some persons is such that it causes us to let them alone, and take no stock whatsoever in their business propositions. Others, instead, imbue us with confidence and trust, and give us the feeling that we would like to do business with them. Some persons leave upon us the impression that we

have been in the presence of a snaky thing,
and we often can scarce repress a shudder of
disgust and dislike; while others create in us
the impression that the other person is a good
friend and can be depended upon as a helper
and comrade. Why? It is not from anything
these persons have said, for, as we all know,
some of the slipperiest persons are often the
smoothest talkers; and some of the best and
most dependable persons are often very reti-
cent, and even "short" in speech. The reason
lies deeper than words. It is the "feeling" that
we experience when we come in contact with
persons, rather than any report of the reason
regarding them. And this "feeling" is caused
by the registry upon our sensitive brain organism of the thought-vibrations of the other
person's personal atmosphere.

Not only are these things noticed in the person himself or herself, but even the very resi-
dences, stores or other places frequented by
the individual are also affected by the continu-
ous influence of the thought-vibrations of his
or her personal atmosphere. Did you ever notice how some houses produce upon you a feeling of sadness or woe, or worse; while others
seem to carry within them an air of health and

good-cheer, happiness and content? This is often true although the house may have been unoccupied for some time, so strong were the mental vibrations of the atmosphere of the person or persons formerly inhabiting them. In the same way some offices and places of business are so saturated with the vibrations of the personal atmospheres of their occupants, that one is forcibly impressed by the same upon entering the door. A man may disguise his thoughts by his words or his facial expression, but the mental vibrations of his personal atmosphere will frequently "give him away." These are facts which should require no further proof—your own experience should be proof enough to satisfy you. But you should make a mental note of this fact, and carry it in mind as we proceed.

Many persons leave but little impression upon us, for the reason that their mental states are so varied, inconstant and fleeting that they neutralize each other, and fail to impart a definite shade of thought-color to the personal atmosphere. The strongest personal atmospheres are those of persons of strong feelings, desires and emotions, good or bad, for such have strong and constant mental states which impress themselves forcibly upon their personal atmospheres, so strongly, in fact, that one who notices these things cannot fail to perceive them.

A moment's thought will inform you that if these things be true—and true you will realize they must be when you give the matter a moment's careful thought—then one should be very careful to avoid harboring mental states of a character likely to inspire undesirable feelings in other persons. And, at the same time, one should endeavor to cultivate mental states of a character likely to awaken feelings of a desirable character in those with whom we come in contact. In fact, a great portion of the following chapters will be usde to teach you how to cultivate just such mental states, so as to create the desired effect upon others, for in this lies one of the great secrets of personal magnetism.

One need not despair if he has been creating and carrying around with him a personal atmosphere of an undesirable kind. For these things may be remedied, and one may entirely change the character of his mental states, and thus transform his personal atmosphere from the very worst to the very best. These things require work, perseverence, and patience, it is true, but the reward is so great that it pays anyone to devote his attention and time to it. The principle is very simple, indeed, but it requires determination and dogged will to obtain the best results, particularly in cases where very undesirable conditions have existed.

The second way in which the mental phase of personal magnetism operates, i. e., that of the conscious projection of the mental currents from the brain centres, by the action of the will of the individual, also demands work on the part of the student who wishes to create a strong personal atmosphere.

The principle of this second form of mental action consists in the use of the will in a conscious projection of thought-currents. This is true in the case of stimulating the personal atmosphere, and also in cases in which one endeavors to produce an effect upon the mind of some other person in whose presence he may happen to be.

While it is true that the character of the mental states of the person will color and give character to his personal atmosphere, which will, of course, produce an effect upon the other person or persons in his field of action, it is likewise true that the effect of such mental vibrations may be enormously increased by the use of the will in the direction of the conscious projection just referred to. The mental states produce and create the mental atmosphere, it is true, but the will serves to project them forth with force, and to generally energize the atmosphere and increase the effect.

It is just as if you had created a great store of mental magnetism in your brain, and given it the proper quality and color by the character of your mental states. This would naturally create a personal atmosphere or aura around you which would be felt by others. But then imagine the increased strength and effect that would arise from the use of your will to **project and force outward** from your brain these mental vibrations. You will see at once how such an action of the will would tend to energize and increase the vibrations of your mental atmosphere, can you not? It would be like turning on an extra force of the power, would it not? Certainly it would, and you may gain this effect whenever you wish to do so, by using the methods which will be given you in this book as we proceed.

Again, you will see, by a little thought, how much stronger will be the effect upon any special individual, if, in addition to the vibrations of our personal atmosphere, we add the force of a special current of mental force directed steadily and pointedly at his mind, by an effort of our will. Do you see the point? You first affect him by the effect of your energized personal atmosphere, and then just when he is in the proper receptive condition you discharge at him a psychic rifle-ball which hits him right in the bull's eye of his mind with enormous force.

At first thought, this may seem to you like a very strenuous proceeding, and one which would require the outlay of a great amount of will-power on your own part. But, this is not so, for the thought-currents are very responsive to the action of the will, and the main thing is to hold the will firmly to the task, and the thought-currents will flow out over the channel thus made for them. It is like holding a rifle properly aimed, and then letting the force of the powder drive the bullet home; or, again, like holding the nozzle of a hose pointed exactly where you wish the current of water to go, and lo!! when the water is turned on, it flies straight to the mark, long after it has left the tip of the nozzle of the hose.

The strong men of all times have employed the will in this way in the direction of creating a strong personal atmosphere, and also in the direction of producing a strong impression upon those who they wished to effect. In many cases they have not fully understood the character of the forces set into operation by themselves, but they understood the "how" part, even if they did not grasp the ' why." The next time you come in contact with a strong individual, watch him or her, and see if you cannot almost see the operation of this direction of mental force of which I have just spoken. But, far more important than even studying others, is that of cultivating the art of doing the thing for yourself, and this is what I am trying to teach you to do. And you will succeed in it, too, if you will enter into the work fully with heart and mind. Get in earnest about it, and the power will develop in you to bring about success.

CHAPTER IV.

THE PHYSICAL PHASE.

The physical phase of personal magnetism depends upon two coordinated manifestations of nerve-force, as follows: (1) the generation within the nervous system of a plenteous supply of nerve-force; and (2) the conscious projection, by the will, of that supply of nerve-force into the personal atmosphere, and even to a greater distance under special conditions.

By "nerve-force," as used in the above paragraph, I mean that strange, mysterious form of energy, which controls all physical movements, and yet, at the same time, appears to be something higher than physical itself. It is akin to electricity or magnetism, in its real nature, and, like these forces is impossible to define. Nerve-force is something far different from the matter of which the nervous system is composed. The nervous system, from spinal-cord to the most delicate nerve filament, is at the best but a system of wires, relays, etc., over which the nerve-force travels, or, else complicated reservoirs in which the nerve-force is stored.

The ordinary nerves serve as wires and cables over which the nerve-force travels to move the parts of the body which we will to move, or which our subconscious mentality desires to move. Certain parts of the brain are great reservoirs of nerve-force, as are also the great groups of nerve-matter called the plexi, prominent among which are the solar plexus, and the sacral plexus.

The ordinary text-books of physiology pass over the question of the real nature of nerve-force, for their writers do not possess the secret. They dispose of the question by saying: "As in the case of electricity, while we fully recognize its existence and its power, nevertheless, we do not know its real nature." And, so, the student must go back to some of the old occult writers of the past ages, and their followers in the present age, in order to get the secret.

All occultists, ancient and modern, have recognized the existence of a mighty subtle force of nature—one of nature's "finer forces"—which is most potent in its effects and activities, but which, nevertheless, defied all power of analysis or definition. The reason that science has never been able to classify nerve-force is because, like electricity, it is in a class by itself, and is different from any other form of force—so different that it cannot be classified with other forces. Science, in some cases, has endeavored to treat it as a secretion of the nervous matter, but that is a folly akin to that of the materialistic philosopher who tried to define mind as "a secretion of the brain," just as the bile is a secretion of the liver, the gall a secretion of the gall-bladder, etc. Such attempts at definition cause only a smile on the face of the wise.

The occulists, on the contrary, while not attempting to define nerve-force (recognizing it to be in a class of its own) nevertheless have discovered the source of its origin, and have given us valuable information as to its use. They have given it many names, as for instance: "vital force," "vital energy," "life force," "vital fluid," "vital magnetism," etc., and in the case of the Orientals, the terms "prana," or "akaschic energy" have been applied to it. But under all of these different names, the occultists have always meant the one and same thing, i. e., nerve-force. The name I use in describing it, "nerve-force," is employed simply because it is found specialized in the nervous system, and not becuase of any idea that it originates there. Indeed, as you shall see in a moment, it has a far higher and more elementary source of origin.

The old materialistic school of physiology has attempted to show that nerve-force, like the bodily material, is derived from the food we eat, and is created by chemical combustion of the latter. This, however, is only partly true. While it is true that there is a certain amount of nerve-force in fresh food (having been gathered there during the life of the plant or animal of which the food formed a part), and while it is true that a certain amount of this nerve-force is taken up by the system of the person eating the food, particularly if the food be fresh, nevertheless, the amount of nerve-force so absorbed is comparatively small, and is far too little to supply what is needed by the individual to run his physical organism. And, even the small part so obtained is not derived from the chemical combustion of the food. Food chemical combustion results in giving bodily heat, but never in creating nerve-force.

The true source of nerve-force, is the same as the source of electricity, namely the universal ether which fills space. Like electricity, also, this force is available to human wants only when it is associated with the atmosphere surrounding the earth. The atmosphere is charged with nerve-force which is taken up and absorbed by the nervous system, and stored away in its great reservoirs, from whence, in turn, it flows over the nerves when required, by the physical or mental needs of the individual.

But, you naturally ask, how does the body absorb the universal nerve-force—through what channel does it enter the system. The answer is plain, viz: In plant, animal and human life, the nerve force is **breathed** into the system. In other words, the process of breathing, in its higher and lower forms, is not alone that of extracting oxygen or other elements from the air, but also that of extracting the universal nerve-force at the same time. When this is understood, it will be more easily understood why the living thing perishes so soon if the process of breathing be interfered with.

The understanding of this secret of nature throws a much needed light upon the important part played by breathing, in the life of all creatures.

Before proceeding to a further consideration of the process of the absorption of nerve-force from the atmosphere, especially in the case of the student of personal magnetism, I ask you to consider another important question in relation to the physical phase of personal magnetism, namely, that of the projection of nerve-force beyond the limits of the nervous system.

You will remember that the average physiologist maintains that it is folly to hold that nerve-force can possibly pass beyond the limits of the nervous system containing it. He holds that, like electricity on the wires, it cannot pass except over the wires of the nerves. But, is this true even of electricity? I positively assert that it is not. The veriest novice in the study of electricity is aware that electricity will leap from one conducting substance to another—jumping the gap in the shape of a spark—and then flying along the new channel. Again, even without the spark, electricity and magnetism will often affect other substances by what is known as "induction," without the actual contact of the two conducting materials. This is so common that it is a wonder that the question is ever raised. And, what is true of electricity and magnetism, in this respect, is likewise true of nerve-force. for it will not only often leap over the barriers of the nervous system, but will, and constantly does, affect other nervous systems by a kind of "induction". Not only is the phenomena of personal magnetism a proof of this transmission of nerve-force, but the phenomena of "human magnetism" (as it has been called) in the direction of "magnetic healing" another proof— a proof, moreover, that may be obtained by any Individual in his own experience.

Moreover, the experience of every individual will bear ample and generous testimony to the fact that certain persons, flowing over with vigorous nerve-force, will so radiate the energy that it is actually perceptible to those shaking hands with them, or even coming into their immediate vicinity. These individuals fairly radiate health and vigor, and exert a postive healing and invigorating effect upon those with whom they come in contact. In a similar manner, is manifested a lack of sufficient nerve-force, by those unfortunate individuals who go around unconsciously absorbing the nerve-force of others, and, in extreme cases, becoming actual vampires sucking the vital forces from those around them. Who of you have not met this last class of persons, and have not noted how depressed and weakened one is after having been in the company of such persons for some time? The average person does not need any further proof in this case, beyond that afforded by his or her own experience.

It may be asked that if the nerve-force is inherent in the universal ether, and obtained from the atmosphere, why all persons are not equally endowed with this energy. The answer is that the life-habits of individuals differ, and just as one is physically strong and robust, and another weak and delicate, so is one individual strong in nerve-force, and another weak in it. Moreover, a change in the life habits of the person will inevitably result in a change in the amount of nerve-force absorbed and retained by him or her. In fact, one of the purposes of this book is to instruct you how you may increase the nerve-force within yourself. While the object is the increase of your personal magnetism, you will find that at the same time your general health and vigor will improve.

In addition to the amount of nerve-force being determined by the life habits of the individual, it is also true that the individual may,
by the proper exercises, so "energize" his nervous system that he will largely increase the
degree of activity of his nerve-force, and may
render it far more available for his requirements. It is not only a question of securing a
plenteous supply of nerve-force, but also of
having the same in an active condition, and in
such a form that it may be readily available for
the requirements of everyday life.

CHAPTER V.

PHYSICAL MAGNETISM

You will remember that when you have come in contact with any of the strong characters in any walk of life—the great preachers, lawyers, statesmen, orators, business men, etc.—those whose success depends upon the strong effect they produce upon other persons,—you have been conscious of a feeling that they radiate **strength** and power. You actually **felt** the power coming from them. And, you will also remember that this power did not seem to you to be mental power, or intellectual strength alone—it seemed, instead, to have much of the physical in it. So strong is this power in the case of some of the world's great characters, that they seem to be personified will-power—mighty centres of vitalized energy, affecting all with whom they come in contact.

In order to realize the difference between this power and pure intellectual strength and ability, you have but to remember another class of gifted persons, namely, the great students, writers, etc., and other men who have developed great intellectual power. These men as a rule are not "magnetic," as the term is generally used. They do not radiate or throw off force, and the element of physical magnetism is almost entirely absent. They seem to be centres of great intellectual energy—but nothing more. I am not now speaking of individuals in whom both the intellectual and the physical are well balanced and combined, but instead, of those individuals who are distinctly "mental" or intellectual. A moment's thought will recall many examples of the type to which I refer—the teachers, preachers, lawyers, and students whose intellectuality is well developed, but who lack that "something" which impresses persons.

Another appeal to your memory will show you, also, that the "magnetic" person is almost always possessed of that indefinable something which we call "strength" and energy. He may not be a stout, large person—he may even be a scrawny, lank individual, of slight frame and small stature—but, even in the last case he will be "wiry" and like a coiled wire spring, full of latent energy. The magnetic person is never the weak, flabby, jelly-fish type. I have seen these thin magnetic persons on their death-beds, weakened by disease, but even in their last moments they gave one the impression of keen spring-like strength. The other type of magnetic person, the stout type, also gives the impression of power and strength—a something within which stores and radiates strength and power. Is this not so in your own experience? Did you ever see a great leader—a magnetic personality—who did not convey the idea of "strength" in the physical sense? I think not.

Now, remember, that I am not claiming that physical nerve-force alone constitutes personal magnetism. Far from this—there are many men who possess and radiate physical nerve-force who are not personally magnetic in the full sense of the term. The combination of mental magnetism, and physical magnetism is needed to produce the full phenomenon of personal magnetism, remember. But, I do insist that mental magnetism without its physical counterpart, is like a mind with a body—it lacks substance and effectiveness.

The occulists inform us that in the personal

atmosphere of the individual—his "aura," they call it—there is to be found not only the vibrations of his mental states and character, but also the vibrations of his physcal magnetism, or nerve- force as I have called it in this book. They state that to those who have developed psychic or clarivoyant power, these nerve-force vibrations may be seen extending from the body some two or three feet in either direction, the whole aura having an egg-shape,hence its name. It is said to have a faint violet color— something like a pale electric flame—and to quiver and vibrate in a manner similar to the motions of heated air arising from a stove, or the ground on a hot summer day, so familiar to every observer. They also claim that when a strong person is using his will, this nerve-force, carrying with it his mental magnetism, may be seen shooting in great sheets or flashes from him to the other person or persons. I do not claim to possess this psychic vision myself, but the testimony of many of my psychic friends agree in this matter, and are in accord with the writings of the older occultists. And, at any rate, anyone experimenting with personal magnetism will be convinced that nerve-force or physical magnetism does act in just the way described, though it remain unseen by the eye of the ordinary person.

Another important bit of information furnished by the occultists which is fully verified by my own observations and experiments, and which in fact forms one of the foundation pillars of my system of personal magnetism, is that concerning the part played by nerve-force in the phenomena of telepathy, hynotism, mental influence, and similar phenomena in which the mind of one person acts upon the mind of another—this of course being one of the main features of personal magnetism. I allude to what may be called the "vitalizing" of the thought-waves by the current of nerve-force which is projected at the same time with it.

Thought-waves unaccompanied by currents of nerve-force lack force and effect, and are like cold mental power devoid of life and activity. You will grasp this idea better by reference to a common occurrence, for instance, you have heard many a sermon, speech, or recitation delivered by a person having marked intellectual ability, and filled with good sound thoughts—and yet the delivery seemed dead, dull, colorless and lifeless, did it not? It lacked the life, vigor, and vim of the delivery of some other speaker of even less intellectual power, did it not? And, you have noticed that the personality of some admittedly intellectual personage lacked "life"; while some other less gifted personality fairly radiated life and strength, and consequently, magnetic power. Well, this represents the difference between plain thought-waves, and thought-waves accompanied by strong nerve-force. The one lacks "body" and vitalizing force, while the other possesses this in abundance. Think over this carefully, until you "get it"—for in it lies one of the two great secrets of perosnal magnetism.

A person in whom nerve-force is actively present, and who has consciously or unconsciously acquired the art of combining it with his thought-waves, will send forth words or thoughts fairly charged with dynamic force, reaching and affecting those with whom they come in contact. Like a high-power explosive shell, the nerve-force drives the thought-wave like a bullet to its mark, hitting the bull's eye with a tremendous impact, and making a powerful impression on the mind of the other person or persons. There are persons whose words seem fairly alive, so vital is their action upon the minds of others—these persons have strongly active nerve-force or physical magnetism used in connection with their mental currents. They flash out this combined force toward their audiences of many persons, and the latter are fairly lifted off their feet by the power.

The great leaders of men have had this nerve-force largely developed and actively employed. When they spoke, the other persons were almost compelled to do the bidding of the strong person. Julius Caesar and Napoleon Bonaparte were two marked examples of the use of this power, but, as a fact, every man who sways, moves and rules other persons, is an example worthy of study. The student should, if possible, manage to be thrown in contact with this class of persons, so that he may see, or rather **feel,** for himself, the effect of this mighty force emanating from these individuals. He will then better realize just what part nerve-force plays in the matter of personal influence, and personal magnetism, and then be more firmly resolved to develop it in himself or herself.

There are some persons who seem, naturally, to absorb, store up and effectively use their nerve-force or physical magnetism. Such are very fortunate, for they are saved the trouble of cultivating the processes referred to. But those who do not possess this gift, naturally, may by practice and perseverance develop it in themselves. Nay, more, they may, eventually, even surpass the naturally-gifted man, for the latter does not understand the source or nature of his power, and is apt to neglect or abuse it, while the person who develops it in himself, according to rule, and with a full understanding, has the thing "on tap" as it were, and can always recuperate from an over drain on a nervous system. Knowledge is power, and a cultivated and developed faculty is often far more effective than a similar faculty present at birth, and not understood or worked for.

Beginning with the next chapter, I purpose giving you plain, simple directions for the increase of your nerve-force, the storing up of the same, and the conscious projection of it to vitalize your mental currents. The process is quite natural, and does not partake of any mystic ceremonies or anything of that sort. It is based on purely physiological principles, and is in full accord with natural laws.   When you have once acquired the art and science of the absorption and storing of nerve-force, you will be surprised that you have never thought of it before.

When you acquire this power, you will be conscious of being a centre of an enormous energy, and will also be made aware of your power by the effect upon other persons. Not only in the matter of personal magnetism, I mean, but also in the matter of imparting the vibrations of strength and energy. You will notice that other persons will be conscious of something in your hand-shake and touch that will surprise them. They will not understand just what affects them, but they will be conscious of some strange feeling pervading them. The best plan will be for you to keep your secret to yourself, and to avoid any impression of being out of the ordinary. You wish to create confidence, not fear—and the strange and mysterious causes fear rather than confidence. So keep your own secrets.

CHAPTER VI.

GENERATING NERVE-FORCE.

By reference to the first paragraph of Chapter IV, you will see that I have separated the physical phase of mental magnetism into two coordinated manifestations, the first of which, i. e., the generation within the nervous system of a plenteous supply of nerve-force, I shall now describe.

The word "generation," in this connection, only imperfectly conveys the idea of the actual process of acquiring nerve-force within the nervous system, for the process is one of "absorption" and "distribution," rather than one of "generation." But as the latter term conveys a more simple picture of the process, I have thought well to use it in this connection, particularly as many of the old occult writers have used it, in this sense, before my time.

This process of nerve-force generation may be said to consist of two distinct, yet coordi-

nated phases, viz: (a) the absorption of an
extra amount of nerve-force from the atmosphere, by special forms of breathing; and
(b) the distribution of the same to the great
centres of the nervous system which act as
reservoirs of nerve-force. I shall now proceed to consider these two respective phases,
in their proper order.

The first phase of nerve-force generation
consists of the absorption of an extra supply
of nerve-force from the atmosphere, by means
of special forms of breathing. All persons
constantly absorb nerve-force from the atmosphere, in the ordinary process of breathing, the amount differing with the individual,
or rather, with his habits of breathing. You
will have noticed that the vigorous, strong
individual, nearly always breathes fully—
that is, deep and regularly—while the weak
person will breathe only partially and irregu-
larly. There is a very close connection between full, regular breathing and general
physical health and strength, but I shall not
touch upon this phase of the subject here,
for it forms no part of this special instruction. I merely drop a hint, which the wise
will take advantage of.

Without wishing to lead you into the sub-
tleties of Oriental psychology, with its complicated forms of breathing for psychic and
spiritual development, etc., I must call your
attention, at this point, to the philosophy
underlying some of the Oriental breathing
practices, for the same is based on the sound-
est scientific principles. The Oriental philosophy teaches that each mental and physical
state of the individual is represented by a
special rhythm of breath, the rhythm and
condition always being found together. The
mental or physical condition will invariably
manifest the particular rhythm of breath
which belongs to it; and, likewise (and this
is one of the occult secrets) the deliberate
assumption of a particular rhythm of breath
will speedily result in the manifestation of
the appropriate physical or mental condition.

You have but to consider the subject for
a moment, to see that when you are fright-
ened or angry, you breathe with a different
rhythm than when you are calm and peaceful. Each emotion, up and down the scale,
has its own appropriate rhythm of breath
which invariably manifests at the same time.

Moreover, different physical conditions likewise manifest in coordinated breath-rhythms. Keep a close watch on yourself, and those around you, and you will soon see that the above statements of facts are strictly correct. You will wonder why you never noticed the phenomena before.

A little less known, even, is the correlated fact that the deliberate assumption or "acting out" of the particular breath-rhythm related to a particular emotion, will result in a speedy experiencing of the emotion itself. This also may be tested out on yourself.

You will find that a few moments anger-breath or fear-breath (if well acted out, or assumed faithfully) will result in you soon experiencing a feeling of anger or fear, as the case may be. Likewise, you will find that the breath-rythm of peace, calm, self-control, will be sufficient to induce that particular state of feeling in you.

There is a big hint in this last sentence, by the way, for that is exactly what the Oriental sages do to induce and maintain the mental state of philosophic calm for which they are noted. In this connection, let us

remind you that when you are endeavoring
to control your temper, and to maintain your
poise, under extreme provocation, you will
find that you instinctively strive to control
your breath-rhythm which shows a marked
tendency to fly off into a state of rapid panting and gasping. And, so long as you can
maintain your steady controlled rhythm of
breath, you will maintain your poise and self-
control.

Well, to make a long story short—to get
right down to the gist of the subject of the
absorption of nerve-force through controlled
breath-rhythm—let me say to you (1) that
there is a breath-rhythm which nature uses
to restore nerve force to the depleted system, after a great demand upon it in the direction of either a strong mental or emotional
strain, or after a severe physical strain; and
(2) that a deliberate assumption or "acting
out" of this particular breath-rhythm will
result in your being able to quickly absorb
a greatly increased supply of nerve-force for
the purpose of use in personal magnetism—
to render you full of physical magnetism, in
fact. Do you catch this point? If not, re-
read the above paragraph, several times, until

you fully grasp the importance of the statements therein contained—for they comprise exactly one-half of the philosophy of nerve-force generation—and much more besides if you are able to grasp it.

You naturally ask, at this point: "What is this particular breath-rhythm which nature uses to aid us in recuperating, and which may be assumed with such wonderful results?" Very well, let me answer you by asking you another question, namely: "How do you breathe when you begin to recuperate just after a severe emotional, mental or physical strain, when the characteristic first panting breath quiets down?"

If you will consider carefully, you will answer that you generally begin by one or two long drawn out sighing breaths, followed by a period of calm, deliberate, slow, deep breaths. You may not have noticed it, but these last calm, deep breaths are marked by a slow but regular rhythm—as regular, indeed, as the slow swing of the pendulum of a large clock, or the accompanying "tick" thereof. You will find that this slow, regular rhythmic breath continues for some little time, until you feel refreshed and reinvigorated, when the breath will drop into the normal "everyday" rhythm, and the task is over.

Well, **this is exactly the breath-rhythm which, if properly assumed and well "acted-out," will result in drawing to you a greatly increased supply of nerve-force from the universal storehouse of the same, i. e., the atmosphere around you.**

I ask you, student, to pause at this point, and re-read the preceding paragraph. Consider it carefully, roll it over in your mind, until you fully grasp its tremendous significance, and fully make it your own thought. For in those few lines is condensed a statement of wonderful truth which, if taken advantage of, will transform you into a very giant of physical magnetism. Do not proceed with this reading, until you have fully grasped the importance of the information just given you.

But do not imagine that you can jump at once into this great power. You must first gradually acquire the exact rhythm for yourself—for I can do no more than to indicate it to you. I cannot say, "Breathe in just so many seconds; hold the breath just

so many; and then breathe out just so many,"
and so on, as many teachers have done—some
who should have known better, for that matter. For each person has his or her own particular breath-rhythm of this kind, the difference arising from mental or physical forma-
tion and characteristics.

The following is the rule—the only rule—
in the matter: "Ascertain, first, the precise
breath-rhythm which nature has given you
for use in moments of recuperation after extreme mental, emotional or physical strain;
and then, second, practice the same volun-
tarily by assuming, or acting out the mental
and physical conditions producing it, until
the rhythm becomes fixed in your memory,
so that you can easily reproduce it, instinctively, when you wish." Read this rule over
until you thoroughly understand it.

You will find it somewhat difficult to assume or act out the conditions producing
the rhythm, at first, unless you happen to
be a natural or well-trained actor. But keep
trying, until you master it. Practice will
make perfect, in this as in everything else,
remember. Mentally place yourself in the
same vibrations as when you were under some

great strain of mind, emotion or body, in the past; and you will find that the same will be followed by an acting-out of the period of recuperation, with its accompaniment of appropriate breath-rhythm. Each student will manage this in his, or her, own way, and will get the result, if persistent, persevering effort be made.

You will find that the first indication of the recuperating breath-rhythm will usually be a long drawn out sigh, followed by a moment of rest, which, in turn, is followed by an easy, though deep, slow, deliberate succession of in-breathing and out-breathing, in perfect rhythm, which will be accompanied by a feeling of increased strength and vitality, of mind and body—delightful to experience is the feeling of "relief" and fresh vigor, vitality and vim which results from this breath-rhythm.

In practicing this recuperative breath-rhythm for the purpose of resting, gaining strength, or increasing your store of nerve-force, do not fall into the too-common error of **artificial** rhythmic breathing. Do not make the mistake of trying to count the seconds of the breath; or to make the breaths extend out over a particular time, nor to exactly match each other; or to retain the breath any special time; nor to count time between breaths; or anything of that kind. Forget all about the artificial standards, and give yourself up entirely to a peaceful, calm feeling of relief and recuperation, which nature will bestow upon you if you will create the right conditions for the manifestation of her power. Do not be artificial—trust nature to "run the thing" aright, and leave everything in her hands.

Do not bother at this point, to wonder just how many times a day you must practice this exercise in order to gain physical magnetism and absorb nerve-force. That point will be covered in a later chapter, in connection with the accompanying process of nerve-force distribution—the sole thing before you now is to learn how to produce this breath-rhythm, and to practice until you can produce it at will, easily and naturally, without effort or strain—instinctively, in fact. Until you accomplish this, there is no use of your bothering yourself about the succeeding stages.

And, now a word about practicing this step. Do not overdo the thing—make haste slowly. It is a matter of growth and development with you, and you should not try to rush things too rapidly. Let nature proceed to make the process instinctive, and do not fall into the mistake of pulling up the roots of your plant in order to see whether it has grown overnight. It will grow, never fear. You will know when you are on the right track, and will be aware of your progress, by reason of your increasing sense of vigor, vitality and vim.

Remember, finally, that the secret of the whole thing is that you have discovered how nature recuperates the system in times of extreme necessity; and have then learned how to draw upon this source of energy at will, thereby increasing the supply far above the ordinary. It is just as if you had discovered a bottle containing the elixir of energy which kind Mother Nature uses to recuperate you in times of need; and then you had learned that you could partake of the elixir, daily, or whenever you felt like it; and were consequently enabled to increase your energy and vitality far above the average. The comparison or figure of speech is not exaggerated—for in this secret you have indeed discovered the elixir of vitality, vigor and vim; that is, if you use it aright.

CHAPTER VII.

DISTRIBUTING NERVE-FORCE.

In the preceding chapter I have given you general instructions regarding the first phase of nerve-force generation, i. e., the absorption of nerve-force by means of certain forms of rhythmic breathing. I now proceed to the general instruction regarding the second phase of nerve-force generation, namely, the distribution of the absorbed nerve-force to the nervous system, and particularly to the great reservoirs of nerve-force.

This process of nerve-force distribution naturally follows directly after that of nerve-force absorption, the two being coordinated phases of one of nature's recuperative processes. Just as is the process of the recuperative breath-rhythm nature's way of restoring to the system a fresh supply of nerve-force to replace that used in the extraordinary mental, emotional or physical strain preceding it, so is the process of nerve-force absorption another (or twin) method of nature to distribute the absorbed nerve-force to all parts of the body, strengthening and invigorating, vitalizing and stimulating, each and every part of the body, and at the same time storing up in the great reservoirs of the nervous system a reserve supply of nerve-force for times of future need.

Again you ask: "What is nature's way of distributing the absorbed nerve-force, as above stated, which also is the way in which you state students of personal magnetism may distribute their absorbed nerve-force or physical magnetism?" As in the case of the previous question, I answer, "Go to nature herself, and discover her method." Let us then do so.

Investigating nature's method of distributing physical magnetism or nerve-force, what do we find nature doing just after the person is exhausted by mental, emotional or physical exertion—that is, in addition to the peculiar breath-rhythm. Answer: We find, accompanying the long deep sigh preceeding the breath-rhythm, and also, following the rhythmic breathing, a tendency to **"stretch" the muscles of the body.** Not only do we notice this phenomena at such times, but it is also to be observed when we awaken in the morning with a yawn, followed by an instinctive stretching of the muscles. We observe the same thing after we have used up nerve-force in listening, reading, studying, etc.— in fact, in any action which has required concentrated attention. It is always the yawn, the deep sigh, the measured breath, and, finally, the stretching of the muscles.

Now, do not dismiss this matter with a trifling jest, or an amused smile—for this stretching of the muscles is one of nature's most important offices. It is her own favorite way of distributing to all parts of the body the nerve-force being absorbed into the system. It is her own way of sending a vitalizing and invigorating current to the places in which it is needed. And, moreover, if we will take her seriously; examine the meaning of her process; and then intelligently apply the same in our work of developing physical magnetism, we will have gained an important secret of nature, and one which we will not be willing to part with, once it is applied and turned to account.

In the first place this "stretching" is something far more than a manifestation of laziness, weariness, or fatigue. It is an instinctive action resulting from nature's recognition of the need of a fresh supply of nerve-force, and her rush to supply the needed energy. Do not mistake and confuse causes and effects in this matter.

You will notice, in cases of complete "stretching," a twofold motion, viz.: (1) An extension; and (2) a tensing or contraction of the muscles, in the direction of drawing in the extended limbs or parts of the body. Now note this, both of these motions are forms of "tensing" or contracting the muscles. The extension movements result from the tensing or contracting of one set of muscles; the drawing in movements result from the tensing or contracting of the opposing set of muscles. The principal muscles of the body are arranged in opposing sets, one being used to push out, and the other to draw in, the limb or portion of the body You may always count on the presence of these opposing sets of muscles. When in the process of stretching you first extend, and then draw in the limbs, you really are **tensing** both of the opposing sets, in turn. **For what** purpose? Let us see.

Nature's purpose in tensing the opposing muscles, in the above stated case, seems to be that of "squeezing out" something from the muscles. And that is exactly what it is—a squeezing out of something. Of what? Of the old, stale, weakened nerve-force or physical magnetism. Why?—to what end? To the end that the supply of fresh, vital, strong nerve-force or physical magnetism may rush in to take the place thereof.

This is equally true in the case of brain exhaustion, nerve-exhaustion, or muscle-exhaustion—for the brain cells, the nerves themselves, and the muscles, are kept vitalized and invigorated by the same form of energy, coming from the same source. Moreover, the fresh supply of nerve-force pouring into the muscles and cells, from the great nerve-force reservoirs of the nervous system, leave the latter more or less depleted, and cause them to call for a fresh adequate supply from the universal source. In short, the stretching process sets into operation the whole machinery of the distribution of the system's supply of nerve-force, and results in the whole nervous mechanism being given a new impetus.

This is the secret of the personal magnetism adept's method of distributing a fresh supply of physical magnetism or nerve-force to all parts of the system, at will—thus rendering himself a veritable dynamo of physical magnetism, if he so desires.

But there is more to this method of the student than mere ordinary "stretching," I assure you. The ordinary stretching is simply an elementary form of nerve-force distribution. I shall call your attention to an extension of, and improvement upon, the elementary method.

You have probably heard of that form of calisthenics generally known as "the tensing exercises." Well, in that system you may find the seed of a much more efficient system. The tensing system of calisthenics is taught for the purpose of exercising the muscles— only this and nothing more. It has been found to bring about the greatest results, and to greatly develop the muscles and benefit the general system. Why? "Oh just exercise" replies the physical culturist. But we know better, for while we realize the benefit obtained from these sensible exercises, alone, we also understand how such a rational course of exercise must result in greatly invigorating the entire system, by distributing the nerve-force, and as a consequence bringing about the absorption of a fresh supply to the great reservoir centres of the nervous system, do we not?

We have three decided points of advantage over the "tensing exercise" school, as follows: (1) We precede our tensing exercises by rhythmic breathing exercises, thus bringing to our reservoirs a fresh supply of magnetism or nerve-force; (2) we proceed leisurely and almost "lazily," our idea being that of "stretching" as opposed to the idea of vigorous exercise by tensing, the latter being held by the "tensing exercise" school; and (3) we understand the real reason for the tensing, and hence are able to apply it intelligently, instead of in a hit-or-miss style.

The addition of the rhythmic breath, of course, gives a new and novel impetus to the work of nerve-force distribution; in fact the latter cannot be perfectly performed without the former. This the ordinary tensing exercise practitioner almost entirely misses, except in so far as he becomes fatigued by his vigorous exercise, and is forced to breathe rhythmically, as a consequence, thereby un consciously obtaining at least some of the benefits of the rhythmic breath. The ordinary tensing exercise student, once given our key of the rhythmic breath, is enabled to attain results impossible to him before. He sees a great light, as a consequence.

My students of personal magnetism proceed about the exercises for distribution of nerve-force, or physical magnetism, in an entirely different manner from that of the ordinary practitioner of the tensing exercise systems. The latter work themselves into an exhausted condition, under the belief that their muscles will become better developed by such vigorous exercise. As a consequence, many of them wear out as much as they acquire, of muscular development. My students, instead, pursue anything but a strenuous course of exercising in tensing. Instead of moving vigorously, they proceed slowly, calmly and almost "lazily" in tensing the muscles, in turn extending and then drawing in. They keep before them, all the time, nature's own processes of "stretching," and model their movements entirely upon the same. In this way, as a consequence, there is no exhaustion or using up of nerve-force or tissue to any marked extent, but, on the contrary, there is a constant taking in and distribution of magnetism from the centres to the parts, and consequently a marked increase in vigor, vitality and vim. The difference can be understood perfectly only when one practices my exercises for himself or herself.

Finally, it follows that a much greater effort is obtained by one who practices any form of exercises, understandingly, and with a full knowledge of the "why" as well as the "how" of the thing—of the theory as well as the practice. When one knows just what he is about, and just what he wishes and expects to obtain, then he has gained half of the battle. Lacking this knowledge, he wastes energy and effort, and does much that had better be left undone, while leaving undone much that should be done. Verily, "knowledge is power" in this case, as in many others.

It is somewhat amusing, though sad, to see these "tensing exercise" people using themselves up in vigorous exercising, and, at the same time, losing nine-tenths of the benefits gained by those practicing the "lazy" stretching exercises, accompanied by the **rhythmic** breath, as taught to my students.

CHAPTER VIII.

NERVE-FORCE EXERCISES.

I shall now instruct you in the direction of certain forms of exercise designed to generate nerve-force, or physical magnetism, both in the phase of absorption and that of distribution, according to the general principles set forth in the preceding chapters.

Absorption. The exercises, themselves, are designed to give a free and full distribution to the nerve-force or physical magnetism, but the student must always remember that before the nerve-force may be distributed it must first be absorbed. The absorption, of course, is performed by means of the breath-rhythm, according to the instruction already given you. IMPORTANT: Remember that every series of distribution exercises must be preceded, and followed, by the practice of the rhythmic breath for a few moments. It will also be found beneficial and useful to interject a short period of rhythmic breathing in between these exercises, from time to time. You will soon discover the need of this, from your own feelings. After you have gained familiarity and ease in practicing the distribution exercises, you will find yourself becoming very sensitive to the inflow of the nerve-force during the breath-rhythm exercise, and in a short time will know by your feelings exactly when you need to absorb more nerve-force during the exercise.

At this point I wish to again remind the student that one of the main features of my nerve-force exercises is that of the entire absence of artificiality, and the presence of "naturalness." I do not give set forms of breathing, to be practiced just so often, for so many minutes at a time. Instead, I give the general principles of the method—the "why" as well as the "how"—and then bid the student to be governed entirely by his own instincts in the matter of the duration of exercises, and frequency of the same.

After a short time the student will fall into the natural habit, just as he does into the habits of eating and drinking, and he will know exactly when he should practice nerve-force generation, and how long he should continue the exercise.

Keep the words **"Be Natural'** before your mind, and you will make no mistake. Never overdo the exercises, or force yourself to perform them when you do not feel like it. Avoid anything approaching artificiality in the matter. Some times you may go a long time without practicing and again you may feel the need of the same very often—in either case follow nature's urgings. Again, you may feel like taking but a moment's exercises at a time—like taking a sip of water; while on other occasions you will feel like taking a long spell of exercise—like taking a deep draught of water when you happen to be very thirsty—follow nature in both instances.

STRETCHING EXERCISE. I will begin by calling your attention to a form of exercise which consists of intelligent simple "stretching," but which form of exercise will be found very beneficial. There are a variety of forms of this exercise. I will give you a few general forms, and you may then enlarge on these, and invent combinations, variations, etc.

1. Lying on your back, extend your arms upward over your head, to their full extent

stretch them out easily but thoroughly as far as they will go. Then slowly pull them in. Repeat several times.

II. Stretch the arms sideways from the body—out and then in, several times.

III. Stretch the legs in the same way, several times.

IV. Stretch the neck several times.

V. Stretch the hands and fingers, by moving the hands backward and forward from the wrist; clenching and unclenching the fist; opening and closing the fingers.

VI. Stretch the feet and toes, in the same general manner as in the case of the hands and fingers.

VII. Turn over and lie on your stomach, with the face down on the pillow or floor, and repeat the above exercise in this position. This will bring into play a number of muscles not employed in the former position.

VIII. Rise to your feet and stand with the legs spread out, the feet several feet apart, with arms extended upward and outward. This will oring your body into the general shape of the letter "X". Then rise to your toes and stretch upward as if you were trying to touch the ceiling. Repeat several times.

You will be surprised at the feeling of rest
and renewed strength which will come to you
as the result of the practicing of the above
simple stretching exercises. And yet, simple
as they are, these exercises perform a great
work. You must not lose sight of the fact
that when you tense these muscles, in the act
of stretching and then contracting the limbs,
you really "squeeze out" the old, worn out,
depleted magnetism, and absorb in its place
a fresh supply of vigor, vitality and vim from
the great reservoirs of the nervous system.

Carry in your mind the idea of the sponge,
which in order to absorb fully a supply of
fresh water, must first be thoroughly squeezed
out. The process of the absorption and distribution of nerve-force is very close indeed
to the process of the squeezing-out and re-fill-
ing of the sponge.

The following "tensing exercises" are
really but an extension of the stretching exercises, more elaborate and complicated, but
embodying the same principle. They are useful in energizing the several parts of the body
which are not actively energized by the simple stretching exercises.

Shoulders and Chest. Stand erect; feet

close together; arms at sides. Then draw
forward your shoulders, as far front as they
will go. Hold the position a moment, and
then slowly press the shoulders back as far
as they will go. This will tend to energize
the shoulders and chest. The chest may also
be energized by taking a few deep, full breaths
which will inflate the lungs and thus extend
the chest. The shoulders may also be energized by raising them upward in a "shrug"
and then slowly lowering them to original
position.

Arms, Wrists and Hands. Any simple
exercise which will extend and then contract
the arm-muscles will serve to energize the
arms. Twisting them first one way and then
another will do likewise. Twisting the wrists
and moving the hands loosely backward and
forward from the wrists tends to energize
several very important muscles and nerves
in this part of the body. Clenching and unclenching the hands will energize the hands
and fingers. Spreading out the fingers fan-
shape and then drawing them together will
energize the fingers thoroughly.

Legs, Feet and Toes. Follow the general
idea of the arm and hand exercises, just men-

tioned, in the case of the legs, feet and toes. "Squatting" energizes the thighs. Raising up the toes and then lowering to original position energizes the calves of the legs. The "standing-still run" is a good general leg energizer.

Neck. Move the neck forward, as far as it will go, then backward, as far as it will go; then sideways, to the right, as far as it will go—then to the left in the same way; then twist to the right as far as it will go, then to the left in the same manner. These are splendid neck energizers. There are important nerves running through the neck, which are energized by these exercises.

Twisting and Bending. What may be called "a twisting" of the different parts of the body serves to energize the parts very well indeed. In the same way, "bending" exercises are good. Not only may the legs and arms be twisted easily and effectively, but the entire trunk of the body may be equally effectively betwisted by standing erect with feet, say eight or ten inches apart, toes out, and arms hanging easily by the sides; then easily twisting the body to the right, the neck, trunk and thighs being carried as far as they will go; then twisting to the left in the same manner; repeating several times. Bending the body to the right, then to the left, then forward, then backward, is a good energizer.

In a Nutshell. The foregoing exercises might be elaborated into a book by itself—but what's the use? I have given you in a nutshell the main elements of the exercises, and you may do the elaborating yourself. In fact, I can sum up the general principles of the exercises in three words, viz: STRETCH-ING, TWISTING, BENDING. Think over these three words, and you will see that if you will apply them in every possible way to the various parts of the body, you will have a whole system of tensing exercises at your command, without purchasing expensive text-books on the subject. And, also, remember that in any and all of the so-called "tensing exercises" systems is to be found the best possible principle of nerve-force distribution—always, however, remembering to include the rhythmic breathing according to my previously given instructions. Now, get to work and exercise you ingenuity in devising variations and combinations of the

"stretching, twisting and bending" principles. This will energize your mind as well
as your body.

Energizing the Solar Plexus. The Solar
Plexus lies exactly back of the pit of the
stomach. It may be energized by practicing
a "drawing in" of the abdominal muscles.
This may prove a little difficult at first, but a
little practice will make perfect. Draw the
abdominal muscles "inward and upward"
several times at each exercise.

The Sacral Plexus. The Sacral Plexus is
another important plexus, or great centre of
nerve force. It is located in front of the
lower part of the spinal column—in the region
of the hips. It may be energized by a special
stretching, bending and twisting of that particular region of the body.

In case of impaired vitality or general
weakness, a little extra energizing of these
two plexi may be found very advantageous
and beneficial, as they directly affect large
regions of the body, and important organs.

CHAPTER IX.

PROJECTING NERVE-FORCE.

At the beginning of Chapter IV, I stated that the physical phase of personal magnetism depends upon two coordinated manifestations of nerve-force, namely: (1) The generation of nerve-force; and (2) the conscious projection, by the will, of that supply of nerve-force into the personal atmosphere, and even to a greater distance under special conditions. I have instructed you regarding the phase of nerve-force generation. Let us now consider the second phase, i. e., that of the projection of the same.

Of all of the mental forces of the individual, the *will* is the most powerful, and at the same time the one least understood. It is hard even to define the will. Enough for our purpose to realize that it is the power within the mind whereby man is able to *do things*. Not only does man do the ordinary things of life by means of the will, but he is also able to do some extra-ordinary things when he learns how.

The old occultists fully realized the mighty power of the will of man, and their teachings convey some very valuable information on this subject. One of their teachings was that by the use of his will man is able not only to project thought-waves from his mentality, but that he is also able to consciously project his physical magnetism, or vital energy, in the same way. The discoveries of the most advanced students of the subject, in our times, verify the old teachings of the occultists in this respect. The system I am herein teaching is therefore based not only on the advanced discoveries of modern science, but also upon the world-old teachings of the ancient occultists. Truth knows no special age or time—it is the property of the ages.

The average man projects his physical magnetism, or nerve-force, into his personal atmosphere, or aura, more or less unconsciously—just as he walks or breathes, for that matter. He has naturally acquired the habit, and does not concern himself about the matter—in fact, he is usually unconscious of and ignorant of the process itself.

The differences in the degree of physical magnetism projected or radiated by such persons is determined solely by the degree of nerve-force generated by them, in absence of any special power of projection.

There is a second class, however, the members of which, while not fully informed of their power to project physical magnetism, nevertheless, by their habitual use of the will in the direction of impressing others, powerfully, though unconsciously, direct waves of the nerve-force outward, so that their personal atmosphere becomes well charged with it, and their influence is felt by those coming in contact with it. In this class of individuals will be found the active, energetic. masterful men in various walks of life, who direct others rather than are directed by others, who give orders rather than receive them. These men generally radiate enough physical magnetism to make itself felt by those with whom they come in contact, and are generally felt to be "strong men." But even these persons do not manifest the greatest amount of physical magnetism.

The third class of persons is that composed of individuals who have acquired a greater or less knowledge of the fact that physical magnetism may be projected beyond the limits of the brain or body, and who have learned, at least in a degree, the art of so projecting it by the use of the will. These individuals range from those who have acquired merely a glimpse of the truth, up, by degrees, to those who may be spoken of as Masters of the Art. This last named class of persons are those whose power is readily felt and acknowledged, and who leave their impression upon those who come in contact with them.

The projection of the physical magnetism, by the will, is, in a way, a very simple procedure, consisting of two processes, as follows: (1) The belief in, or realization of, one's powers to so project the force; and (2) the actual willing or commanding the force to be projected.

At first it may seem somewhat strange to learn that "belief" has anything to do with this matter, but a little consideration will explain this general law of psychology. It is this way: The will never acts in a direction which the mind believes impossible. One never tries to reach the moon, because his mind refuses to believe that he can do it—

but the child, believing that it is possible, will use his will to move his hand in that direction. The disbelief acts as a brake on the will—do you see the point?

But, you may say, the belief of the child does not enable him to *reach* the moon. Certainly not, but it caused his will to operate so as to move the hand. Belief does not necessarily render accomplishment certain—but it removes the barriers of disbelief, the latter preventing any accomplishment by the will. There are many things that we would be able to do if we could only believe that we could do—but disbelief acts as a brake and a barrier to the efforts of the will. Realization of one's power will often gain half the battle of accomplishment for him.

In the case before us, the one needs only *to believe enough to make the attempt.* Then, each time the attempt is made, and one perceives a result, the task becomes easier for the next time. And, at last, the sense of full realization of the power of the will dawns upon the person, and after that the rest is easy.

The second process, i. e., the actual willing, or commanding, by the will, is simply what

the words actually say. How can you "will"
or "command" the physical magnetism to
move into your personal atmosphere, and energize it?—will it obey me? you ask. Certainly it will. And the willing or commanding
is simply effort the same that you employ,
instinctively, when you will or command that
your hand be raised. What makes the hand
raise? It has no power to raise itself, neither
have the muscles any such power in themselves. It is only when you WILL it to move,
that things begin to move. The mere *willing*
sends a current of nerve-force over the
nerves, and into the muscles, and the hand
raises. Sounds simple, doesn't it? And yet
it is one of the most wonderful things in the
world—only we have grown so accustomed to
it that we fail to note the wonder of it all.

The command of the will to the physical
magnetism acts in the same manner as the
command of the will to the hand. Now, right
here, is a point to be remembered. You do
not merely say to the hand "raise up." Try
it on your own hand—say to it "raise up"
without actually *willing* it to raise, and nothing happens. It is only when you accompany
the command with the mysterious effort of
the will, that movement occurs.

I cannot tell you how to move your hand by willing—all that I can say is that you must WILL it to raise, and you will understand exactly what I mean. Well, then WILL the physical magnetism to flow out into your personal atmosphere, just as you will the hand to raise, and the thing happens.

But, you may say, you can *see* the hand move, and know whether your command has been obeyed, while you cannot see the physical magnetism flow. Certainly, but you can *feel* the magnetism flow, and thus be certain of it.

The flow of physical magnetism soon becomes perfectly apparent to a person, and he is as certain of his radiation as he is that he is radiating heat on a warm day. It is one of those things which cannot well be explained, but which is readily understood by those who experience it. Try it yourself, and you will soon become conscious of the flow of nerve-force from you, into the field of your personal atmosphere or aura, to a distance of several feet on all sides of you.

You will become aware of the effect of your physical magnetism upon others who come in contact with you. You will be able to per-

ceive the reaction and response to your strong
magnetic influence on them. They will, unconsciously, let you know that they feel the
power of your presence, and acknowledge
your strength. You will find a puzzled expression on the part of some of your old
acquaintances and associates who will be
dimly conscious that there is something different about you which they cannot explain
satisfactorily to themselves. Do not, however,
make the mistake of informing them, for this
will invite unpleasant comment and criticism,
and will also tend to make persons assume a
defensive attitude toward you—and even an
offensive one, perhaps—in self protection.

You will also become aware of the healing
and strengthening effect of your magnetism
upon delicate and sick persons who come in
contact with you. Such persons will feel
strengthened by your presence, and will dislike to leave you. You may experience some
difficulty in preventing them from attaching
themselves to you, and seeking to live on
your magnetism. But when you learn the
art of using the mind-force, or mental magnetism, you will be able to shake them off
when necessary. In the meantime, you may

do much good by giving these persons magnetic treatments, either by consciously directing a stream of magnetism towards them—by
the use of the will—or by the use of the hand.
Your magnetism will flow freely out of your
hands, and will invigorate weak persons,
tend to remove painful conditions, etc. A
little experience will make you a "magnetic
healer" if you should so desire.

In this matter of hand-shaking, you will
notice strange things. Persons who take your
hand will be impressed by something strange
and powerful about you, for your magnetism
will flow out toward them and through their
body, sometimes in a most marked manner,
but more often in an easy current.

You may project your physical magnetism
in a direct current, quite a distance from your
body, by the simple effort of your will, when
once you have learned the little points of
practice by repeated trials.

I shall not speak at this place of the úse
of the physical magnetism in connection with
the mental currents, for that topic will be
taken up in a later chapter, or chapters
rather. But do not wait until that time to
practice—get to work and practice with the

physical magnetism, now, so that you will
have it well in hand when you receive the
higher instruction regarding the mental currents. Plant your feet firmly on each step of
the ladder—then you will not slip when
climbing. Do you see the point?

CHAPTER X.

MENTAL RADIATION.

Leaving for the moment the phase of physical magnetism, or nerve-force, and entering into a consideration of the other phase, namely, that of mental magnetism or thought-force, let us first take a general glance at the report of the most advanced science of the day, upon the subject of the phenomena of mental radiation.

It will be well for you to feel fully convinced of the reality of this phenomena, before you undertake to manifest the power. This not only to maintain consistency and mental honesty on your own part, but also that you may rid yourself of any doubt or unbelief in the matter, the result of such doubt or unbelief being to interpose a barrier or brake upon the will, as we have stated in a preceding chapter.

Listen to the following words from the pen of one of the world's great scientists, Professor Ochorowicz, who has created such a

wonderful stir here in Paris by his demon-
strations of practical psychology, mental
photography, etc. Professor Ochorowicz
says: "Every living being is a dynamic

"A dynamic focus tends ever to propagate
the motion that is proper to it. Propagated
motion becomes transformed according to the
medium it traverses. Motion tends always to
propagate itself."

"Therefore, when we see work of any kind
—mechanical, electrical, nervic, or psychic—
disappear without visible effect, then, of two
things, one happens, either a transmission or
a transformation. Where does the first end,
and where does the second begin?"

"In an identical medium there is only
transmission. In a different medium there is
transformation. You send an electric current through a thick wire. You have the current, but you do not perceive any other force.
But cut that thick wire and connect the ends
by means of a fine wire; the fine wire will
grow hot; there will be a transformation of a
part of the current into *heat*."

"Take a pretty strong current and interpose a wire still more resistant, or a very
thin carbon rod, and the carbon will emit

light."

"A part of the current, then, is transformed into heat and light. This light acts in every direction around about, first visibly as light, then invisibly as heat and electric current."

"Hold a magnet near it. If the magnet is weak and movable, in the form of a magnetic needle, the beam of light will cause it to deviate; if it is strong and immovable, it will in turn cause the beam of light to deviate."

"And all this from a distance, without contact, without special conductors."

"A process that is at once chemical, physical and psychical, goes on in a brain. A complex action of this kind is propagated through the gray matter, as waves are propagated in water. Regarded on its physiological side, an idea is only a vibration, a vibration that is propagated, yet which does not pass out of a medium in which it can exist as such. It is propagated as far as other vibrations allow. It is propagated more widely if it assumes the character which subjectively we call emotive. But it cannot go beyond without being transformed. Nevertheless, like force in general, it cannot remain in isolation, it escapes in disguise."

"Thought stays at home, as the chemical action of a battery remains in the battery; it is represented by its dynamic correlate, called in the case of the battery a current, and in the case of the brain— know not what; but whatever its name may be, it is *the dynamic correlate of thought.* I have chosen the term 'dynamic correlate.' There is something more than that; the universe is neither dead nor void."

"A force that is transmitted meets other forces, and if it is transformed only little by little it usually limits itself to modifying another force at its own cost, though without suffering perceptibly thereby. This is the case particularly with forces that are persistent, concentrated, well seconded by their medium. It is the case with the physiological equilibrium, nervic force, psychic force, ideas, emotions, tendencies. These modify environing forces, without themselves disappearing. They are imperceptibly transformed, and, if the next man is of a nature exceptionally well adapted to them, they gain in inductive action."

Various other eminent scientists have testified to the general resemblance of the brain to an electrical or magnetic battery or cell group. Professor Bain has said: "The structure of the nervous substances, and the experiments made upon the nerves and nerve centres, establish beyond doubt certain peculiarities as belonging to the force that is exercised by the brain. This force is of a current nature; that is to say, a power generated at one part of the structure is conveyed along an intervening substance and discharged at some other part. The different forms of electricity and magnetism have made us familiar with this kind of action."

Professor Draper tells us that: "I find the cerebrum is absolutely analogous in construction to any other nervous arc. It is composed of centripetal and centrifugal fibres, having also registering ganglia. If in other nervous arcs the structure is merely automatic, and can display no phenomena of itself, but requires the influence of an external agent—the optical apparatus inert save under the influence of light, the auditory save under the impression of sound—the cerebrum, being precisely analogous in its elementary structure, pre-supposes the existence of some agent to act through it."

Dr. Haddock says, in connection with his consideration of the idea that thought may be communicated through ether-vibrations: "The ether is accepted by science as a reality, and as a medium for light, heat electricity, magnetism, etc. The nervous system is certainly comparable to an electric battery with connecting wires. Communications of thought and feeling without the mediation of sense-perception as commonly understood, is now established. Inanimate objects exert, now and then, 'strange influences.' People certainly carry with them a personal atmosphere. The representation of the condition of these facts by a psychic field, compared to the magnetic or electric field, becomes, therefore, if not plausible, as least convenient. As such a 'field' exists surrounding the sun, so may a 'field' be assumed as surrounding each human individual. 'We have already strong grounds for believing that we live in a medium which conveys to-and-fro movements to us from the sum, and that these movements are electro-magnetic, and that all the transformation of light and heat, and indeed the phenomena of life, are due to the electrical energy which comes to us across the vacuum which exists between us and the sun—a vacuum which is pervaded by the ether, which is a fit medium for the transmission of electro-magnetic wares.' By means, then, of a similar theory applied to mind and brain and body, we may find reasonable explanations of many otherwise insoluble mysteries of life, and, which is of more importance, deduce certain suggestions for the practical regulation of life in the greatest individual interest.''

Haddock also approvingly quotes the following from Dr. M. P. Hatfield, an authority with whom I, personally, am not familiar: ''The arrangement of the nerve-envelopes is so like that of the best constructed electrical cables that we cannot help thinking that both were constructed to conduct something very much alike. I know that there are those who stoutly maintain that nerve-force is not electricity, and it *is* not, in the sense that an electrical battery is the same thing as a live man; but nevertheless nerve-force is closely allied to that wonderful thing that for the want of a better and clearer understanding we agree to call electricity.''

Haddock adds: ''All states of body and mind involve constant molecular and chemical change. The suggestion arises that the brain, with its millions of cells and its inconceivable changes in substance, may be regarded as a transmitting and receiving battery. The brain being a kind of battery, and the nerves conductors of released stored-energy to different parts of the body, by a kind of action similar to the actions of electricity and magnetism, it is suggested that, either by means of the ether, or of some still finer form of matter, discharges of brain energy may be conducted beyond the limits of the body. If the nerve-track correspond to wires, this refined medium may correspond to the ether-field supposed to be employed in wireless telegraphy. As electrical movements are conducted without wires, or other visible media, so may brain-discharges be conveyed beyond the mechanism of the battery, without the intervention of nerves—except as they may constitute a part of the battery. Generally speaking, such discharges would originate in two ways: by direct mental action, or by mental or physical states—perhaps by a combination.''

In the above quotations, there will be found constant reference to vibrations in the universal ether. That there is a place, and plenty of room, in the scale of etheric vibrations for the vibrations of mental-force, may be seen by a reference to the following quotations from eminent authorities:

Professor Gray has said: "There is much food for speculation in the thought that there exists sound waves that no human ear can hear, and color waves of light that no eye can see. The long, dark, soundless space between 40,000 and 400,000,000,000,000 vibrations per second, and the infinity of range beyond 700,000,000,000,000 vibrations per second, where light ceases, in the universe of motion, makes it possible to indulge in speculation."

Professor Williams has said: "There is no graduation between the most rapid undulations or tremblings that produce our sensation of sound, and the slowest of those which give rise to our sensations of gentlest warmth. There is a huge gap between them, wide enough to include another world of motion, all lying between our world of sound and our world of heat and light. And there is no good reason whatever for supposing that matter is incapable of such intermediate activity, or that such activity may not give rise to intermediate sensations, provided there are organs for taking up and sensifying these movements.''

A recent writer in the London "Post," says: "The knowledge we gain by experiment brings home to us what a miserably imperfect piece of mechanism our bodies are. The ear can detect the slow-footed sound vibrations that come to us at the rate of between 40 and 40,000 a second. But the whole of space may be quivering and palpitating with waves at all sorts of varying speeds, and our senses will tell us nothing of them until we get them coming to us at the inconceivable speed of 400,000,000,000,000 a second, when again we respond to them and appreciate them in the form of light.''

Another writer, an American psychologist, carries on the tale from this point, as follows: "The first indications of warmth comes when the vibrations reach the rate of 35,000,000,-000,000 per second. When the vibrations reach 450,000,000,000,000 the lowest visible light ray manifests. Then comes the orange rays, the golden yellow, the pure yellow, the greenish yellow, the pure green, the greenish blue, the ocean blue, the cyanic blue, the in-

digo, and finally the violet, the highest degree of light which the human eye can register, and which occurs when the vibrations
reach the rate of 750,000,000,000,000 per second. Then come the ultra-violet rays, invisible to human sight, but registered by chemical media. In this ultra-violet region lie the
'X Rays,' and the other recently discovered
high-degree rays; also the actinic rays which,
while invisible to the eye, register on the
photographic plate, sunburn one's face, blis-
ter one's nose, and even cause violent explo-
sions in chemical substances exposed to them,
as well as acting on the green leaves of
plants, causing the chemical change of trans-
forming carbonic acid and water into sugar
and starches. These forms of 'dark light,'
that is, light too fine to be perceived by the
human eye, are but faint indications of the
existence of still higher and finer vibrations
—the 'finer forces of nature.' "

Oh, yes! there is plenty of space and room
in Nature's scale of forces, for the vibrations
of mental energy, nerve-force, and personal
magnetism which combines the two. I trust
that the foregoing statements of scientific
fact have cleared your mind of any lurking
doubts on the subject.

CHAPTER XI.

MENTAL ATTITUDES

In a preceding chapter, I have stated that the mental phase of personal magnetism consists of two coordinated manifestations of mental power, the first of which was "the holding of certain mental states until the mental atmosphere becomes charged with the vibrations of the particular mental states." Let us now consider what are these "certain mental states" which are to be held.

In the first place, these "mental states" are not so much any set of particular thoughts, but rather are stated mental attitudes in relation to oneself and the outer world of men. A man's mental attitude, if firmly defined and as firmly held, impresses itself upon everything around the man. His looks grow to conform; his voice; his walk; his general appearance; all grow to reflect his inner states of mind. Moreover, his mental atmosphere becomes so charged with certain vibrations that those who come in con-

98

tact with the man actually *feel* his mental attitude, and adjust themselves to it.

Who of us cannot recall the "so meek and humble," Uriah Heep mental attitude manifested by some persons of our acquaintance. Who does not remember having actually felt the sneaky, foxy mental attitude of certain other persons. And who can forget the bold, masterful, mental attitude of certain successful men in our field of business acquaintance? Each of these classes is possessed of a mental atmosphere which reveals itself at once to us, when we meet them.

I need scarcely urge upon you the importance of producing in yourself the most desirable kind of personal atmosphere. And, as I have said, the mental atmosphere is the direct result of the mental attitude of the person, and reflects the same inevitably. Of course, the mental attitude of a person is composed of a variety of beliefs, opinions, views, ideals, etc., and must of necessity be of a somewhat mixed character. In the case of the majority of persons, the personal atmosphere lacks force and character because of a lack of any particular mental color. But, in the case of the strong individuals of the race, it will be found that there is always a strong fixed mental attitude—a strong desire which colors all the thought; a powerful ambition which gives tone to all the rest; or a firm resolve which fires the entire mental character. This strong vibration is carried out into the personal atmosphere, and its influence is felt, and men react thereto.

In a general way, mental attitudes may be divided into two classes, viz.: (1) positive; and (2) negative.

It is difficult, at first, to give the keynote of each of these two classes of mental attitude, but I call your attention to the words of an American writer, in this connection who well says: "That which tends to render one strong, is positive; that which tends to render him weak, is negative." I do not think that I can improve on this definition, and I advise you to adopt it, and to measure your mental attitudes by that standard.

By all means cultivate and develop the positives, and restrict the negatives, in your mental make-up—so that, in the end, your mental attitude may be "positive" instead of 'negative"—strong instead of weak.

An interesting thing about the cultivation

of a mental attitude, is that not only does the improved mental attitude tend tc impress itself upon others with whom you come in contact, but that it also tends to impress itself upon your own mentality, so that you gradually become more and more fixed in the mental attitude.

Mental attitude resembles yeast, in the sense that if you insert a single bit of the ferment in your mind, it will begin to work, and grow other cells, until it finally fills your entire mind. It tends to reproduce itself. This is true of both desirable and undesirable mental ideas, but—and remember this well —here is a most hopeful and encouraging fact: *A positive idea will tend to kill a negative one,* so you see Nature is fighting on your side. The best way to kill and destroy negative mental ideas and attitudes, is to plant a good crop of positives in their places, and then encourage the fight—the negatives will go under surely. It is like pouring fresh water into a basin of dirty water—in time the water will become clear; or, again, like flooding a room with sunshine—the darkness will be destroyed.

Let us take a little glance at the principal

positives and negatives, in the list of mental attitudes:

Positives	Negatives
Courage	Fear
Masterfulness	Slavishness
Activity	Sluggishness
Initiative	Waiting-for-Orders
Dynamic Thought	Static Thought
Self-Esteem	Self-Distrust
Assertiveness	Retreat-iveness
Continuity	Fickleness

This list might be extended much further, but I think that you will have caught the idea by this time. Run over the list of the strong positive qualities of the strong men of your acquaintance and endeavor to reproduce them in yourselves. Run over the list of weak, negative qualities of the weak persons you know—and endeavor to "cut them out" of your mental attitudes.

In this work of building-up of mental attitude, remember this: *"The mind grows to resemble that upon which it feeds,"* and therefore, you should "feed" your mind with the very kind of ideas which you would like

to have your mental attitude reflect. For instance, if you desire a mental attitude of
Courage, Determination, Masterfulness, Success, etc., you should read stories in which
these points of character are brought out;
you should frequent the company of this kind
of persons; you should constantly hold in
your mind the IDEAL of the things you wish
to develop in your mental attitude, and you
will find that you will naturally find in the
outer world the material things corresponding to them. And, remember this, avoid the
opposite and negative books, persons and
thoughts, as you would poisonous snakes.

It is astonishing how quickly the mind will
respond to the steadfast holding of the POS-
ITIVE IDEAL, and the stimulating environment of POSITIVE things. In a short time,
there will be set up an instinctive habit of
mind which will select the positive things
from its environment and will also reject
the negative things. Train your mind to
select the right kind of food for itself, and it
will soon acquire the habit and perform the
work instinctively without any special super-
vision on your part. Moreover, there will be
developed in your mind that which that gifted

American writer, Prentice Mulford, once called "The Attractive Power of Thought," by means of which you will draw to yourself the things, persons, books, etc., which will supply you with the particular kind of mental food best fitted to the IDEAL you are carrying in your mind. I shall not discuss this last wonderful phenomenon, but ask you to remember and apply the fact, nevertheless, for it is one of the great forces of nature.

Finally, I advise you to sit down and make a careful, full, and *honest* chart of your mental characteristics, positive and negative. Then, place a plus sign before the positives, and minus sign before the negative. Then every day run over your plus list, and fix in your mind the idea that these positives MUST be developed; and that the negatives MUST be restricted. The development of the positives will come about by the holding in mind of the *ideal* of them—thus they will develop and increase, like a self-multiplying cell. The negatives may be restricted by *developing their opposites*—for, this is the application of the law that positives kill out negatives. Upon these two great fundamental laws of practical psychology, one may build a character at will. I will repeat them once more, so that you will fix them in your mind.

I. Feed your positive qualities by ideas of the same kind, in thoughts, books, persons, environment, etc.

II. Restrict or kill-out your negatives, by developing their positive opposites.

And, now, for a wonderful plan of developing a positive mental attitude. This plan has been successfully practiced by many of my students, some of whom stand high in the list of the world's great men. It is this:

Build up for your own use, an IDEAL PATTERN of that which you wish to be. Map out exactly the characteristics which you wish to be yours. Then picture, in your mind's eye, an individual possessed of just these qualities—a complete model, or pattern, of that which you wish to be. Then hold that pattern or model, constantly in your imagination. See it ever; think always about it; view it from the inside and the outside; get fully acquainted with it. And, gradually you will begin to grow like your ideal. The IDEAL will begin to materialize in your own character, and your mental attitude will be that of your model.

Do not pass by this rule, because of its sim-plicity. It has worked miracles for others—why not for you? If you will persist with this plan, your mental attitude will become positive and fixed, and your personal atmos-phere will be charged with the strong, pos-itive vibrations which will proclaim you as a master.

Let this idea be yours, in studying the fol-lowing chapters, and remember that in this way you can get the best results from the special instruction which is to follow this chapter

CHAPTER XII.

THE MENTAL ATMOSPHERE

Following the consideration of the first manifestation of the mental phase of personal magnetism in the preceding chapter, we naturally reach the second manifestation of the same, namely: "The conscious projection of the mental current from the brain centres, by the action of the will of the individual."

This "conscious projection," in turn, may be said to consist of two forms of manifestation, viz.; (1) the projection into the personal atmosphere; and (2) the projection of a direct current, under special circumstances, into the mind of another person, for the purpose of direct influence upon him or her. Let us consider these two forms, in turn, beginning with the first named.

As to the nature of the process whereby one may project his mental currents into his personal atmosphere, I would say that the method is almost precisely identical with that whereby one projects his physical magnetism, or nerve-force, into his personal atmosphere, as fully set forth in Chapter IX.

As in the case of physical magnetism, is found that the average person colors his personal atmosphere by the character of his mental states, or rather by the predominant color of his mental attitude, without any special effort on his part. The degree of color—not its particular *kind*, remember, but its degree of force—depends upon the degree of mental activity of the person. The person of inactive thought, ideas or feeling, will have an almost colorless personal atmosphere, while the person of the active mind will display a marked degree of thought-color therein.

We find here, also, the second class of persons, who, while not fully understanding the nature of their power, or the processes of projection, nevertheless manifest a high degree of thought color and power in their personal atmosphere. This strong color and power results from the fact that such persons are usually individuals of a high degree of feeling or idealism—that is to say, they experience strong feelings, on the one hand; or else have strong mental ideas of anything in which they are interested—or perhaps both strong feeling and strong idealism.

The strongest color and power manifested by persons of this class, is found in persons who take *a strong interest* in things. This strong interest really combines the two elements of feeling and attention, respectively. Feeling is a strong mental element; and attention, you will remember, is a direct application of the will. So, it follows, that such persons must strongly project their mental states into their personal atmosphere, although unconscious of the same, and without a deliberate employment of the will for this purpose.

But, here, as in the case of the physical magnetism, the strongest and most powerful effect is produced by the individuals who understand the process, and who consciously and deliberately project their thought into their personal atmosphere, where it joins and is vitalized by their physica magnetism, so that its full effect is manifested upon those who may come within its field of influence.

The process of using the will in the direction of projecting thought-color and power into the personal atmosphere is practically

identical with the use of the will in the case
of physical magnetism, or nerve-force, as described in Chapter IX. In other words, it
consists of two phases, viz.: (1) belief in
one's power to so project; and (2) the actual
projection by the will. I have informed
you fully regarding the part played by ''belief'' in this process of projection, and shall
say nothing more on this subject here. The
use of the will in the matter of projection,
here also, consists of the *actual willing or
commanding* of the thing itself.

The mental currents are very obedient to
the will, and in fact, depend almost entirely
upon the will for power to move and act.
And, do not forget this, for it is important,
the will is moved largely by desire. If you
will strongly desire that your personal atmosphere be colored by your thought currents,
and will at the same time picture the thought
currents flowing out and filling your personal
atmosphere, you will have little left to do in
the direction of the conscious use of the will.
This because, in the first place, the will naturally operates along the lines of strong desire; and second, because the forming of the
mental picture will result in the use of the

attention, and the attention, as I have said, is a positive and direct action of the will in the direction of focusing its power. So, you see, by following this plan, you are really setting into operation the power of the will itself, although not by direct command. You may also use the direct command to the will to project the thought currents, just as you use the same to lift your arm or close your eyes.

There is one other important point, though, which you must make note of and actively employ in your work of building up and maintaining a strong positive personal atmosphere. I allude to the process of intermingling and combining the two elements of personal magnetism, i. e., (1) the physical magnetism; and (2) the mental magnetism. While there is a natural combination and intermingling of these two, without any special effort on your part, nevertheless, an enormously greater effect will be obtained by a distinct mental process on your part, in which process is combined the several uses of the will above referred to.

This special process consists of three distinct mental operations, as follows:

(1)   You must earnestly *desire* the combination of the two elements of personal magnetism, the physical and the mental forces. You must create the strongest kind of desire for this combination.   This desire must be stronger than a mere "want"—it must be fanned up to the stage of an actual "longing" or "craving" for the combination in question.   (2) You must use the imagination, actively, in the direction of forming a mental picture of the mingling of the two forms of magnetism, just as you would picture the combination of two clouds, or two currents of water in a lake, flowing in from two different sources.   The stronger and more vivid you can make this picture, the stronger and more effective will be the result.   I have explained that these mental pictures require the use of the attention, and that the attention is due to a direct and concentrated use of the will.   Therefore, the will is actively and powerfully employed in this process, and the result is correspondingly effective.   (3) The direct command of the will itself, in the direction of "willing" the currents to coalesce and combine.   These three phases of the use of the will, combined, will prove very

effective in the direction named. A little
practice will enable you to perform all three
of them, at one time, almost automatically.

You will see, by a little thought, that the
process just described, is practically that
used when you perform any conscious, volun-
tary motion of the body. Let us see: You
wish to raise your hand. What processes are
involved? Three, as follows (1) Desire—
you wish to raise your hand; (2) mental picture—for almost unconsciously you form the
image of the raised hand; and (3) the direct
command of the will, which is the final mental
effort.

The combination of the two forms of personal magnetism, the physical and the mental, works along two lines of action, namely,
(1) the mental magnetism gives color and
character to the physical magnetism; and
(2) the physical magnetism gives vitality
and acting force to the mental magnetism.
It might be said, almost, that the physical
magnetism gives the body and moving force
to the combination; while the mental magnetism gives the "soul" to it. Each re-
doubles the efficiency of the other, by the
power of the combination.

The occultists inform us that the personal atmosphere is composed of certain colors, depending upon the particular quality of mental states that happen to be predominant in the combination—each mental state being said to have its own color. I shall not take up this phase of the subject, but merely mention it because of its general interest in this connection.

The occultists also inform us that, when the combination of the two elements of magnetism combine, the mental magnetism takes on a deeper and more pronounced color and hue, and appears also to solidify and become denser; and that the physical magnetism seems to be rendered doubly active, its increased energy being evidenced by tiny sparks and dancing glittering atoms. It seems to be like the combination of two different chemicals, each tending to increase the potency and activity of the other; and the two combining in the production of particularly potent and active new thing.

From the same sources, we learn that the aura or personal atmosphere of the person who uses the will in the direction of forming the potent combination of the two forms of magnetism, seems to be almost alive, so filled with energy is it. It is said that when it comes in contact with other persons—particularly when the owner is using his mind to impress and influence the others—the aura will reach out, and actually enfold the other persons within its field of energy, seemingly trying to embrace the person and hold him subject to the vibration of its owner's mind.

When you learn to produce this combination effectively, you will begin to notice that you will almost unconsciously affect and influence other persons with whom you come in contact. You will notice that they will begin to take on your moods and general feelings, and that they will fall "in tune" with your mental vibrations, generally. If you are enthusiastic about anything, they will begin to manifest enthusiasm. And so on, each of your mental states registering an effect upon the other persons. Moral: Hold only those mental states which you wish others to "take on." And, keep your inner opinions and designs well to the back of your mind, by an effort of the will, and show only what you wish to be sensed by others, for remember your thought currents will have become wonderfully dynamic and powerful.

CHAPTER XIII.

MAGNETIC CURRENTS

The magnetic energy of the person, formed by a combination of his physical and mental force, like all other forms of magnetic or electric force, tends to run in currents, and to be transmitted in waves. The personal atmosphere of the person is, in fact, composed of many waves of magnetic energy, circling around the confines of his aura, a constant wave-like motion being maintained, and a rapid rate of vibration always being manifested.

It is these waves of magnetic energy which, when coming in contact with the mind of other persons, set up a corresponding rate of vibration there, and thus produce a mental state in them corresponding to that of the person sending forth the magnetism. As I have already stated several times, the physical magnetism gives the "body" 'and energizing quality to this personal magnetism,

116

while the mental magnetism supplies the quality of color or character to it.

At this point I wish to digress for a few moments in order to make clear to your mind the important fact that in charging the mental atmosphere with the combined mental and physical magnetism, it is not necessary to make two distinct and separated efforts of the will. In describing and explaining to you the process of sending forth the currents of physical magnetism, and mental magnetism, respectively, I have been compelled to take up each phase separately, and describe the action of the will in the process of projecting each of these phases of personal magnetism. And, if I were to say no more on this point, the student might be left with the impression that in order to fully charge his personal atmosphere with the combined waves of physical and mental magnetism, he would have to first charge it with one kind of magnetism, and then with the other. This is not correct, for a combined effort of the will is all that is required, as you shall now see.

It is possible to combine the mental picture of the two forms of personal magnetism, the physical and the mental, into one image or idea in the mind. It is also possible to combine the two into the desire or inclination to project the energy. And, it is equally possible to combine the projection of the two into one effort of the will. It is a simple thing —as simple as that of twisting two silk threads; threading them into the eye of a coarse needle; and then taking stitches with the needle. Think of the physical and mental magnetism as two twisted threads inserted into the eye of your needle of will, and then think of your passing these threads together into the fabric, by simply pushing the needle through. This illustration will enable you to form a clearer mental picture of the process.

You will find that after a little practice you will instinctively combine the two threads in the eye of the needle of your will. At first, you may find it easier to first think of the physical magnetism, and then of the mental —so to speak, threading first the one thread and then the other. But after a very little practice you will find it easier to take up the two threads at once, *giving them a little twist together*, and then passing both of them through the eye of the will-needle at the same time. Remember, then, learn to "twist to-

gether'' the threads of the two kinds of magnetism, so that the will may push them both
through at the same time.

You should keep the personal atmosphere
well charged at all times, by projecting magnetism into it several times a day. No special
times or number of times is absolutely necessary—you must use your own judgment and
feelings in this matter. You will soon learn
to feel when your magnetic aura is weak, and
when it is strong. These things come to one
by practice and actual experience, and cannot very well be taught except through actual
experience. You will soon learn what it is to
''feel'' the condition of your magnetism, just
as you now feel heat or humidity, or the reverse thereof.

If you are about to come into contact with
others whom you wish to influence; or, on the
other hand, if you are about to come in contact with others who may want to influence
you; you should charge yourself well with
magnetism—that is to say, you should generate and project into your personal atmosphere a large amount of magnetism, which
will thus render your aura strong and positive, instead of weak and negative. The prin-

cipal thing in battle is to be fully prepared for any emergency, and this rule is applicable to the case of the use of personal magnetism in your dealings with other persons.

Remember, then, to combine the idea and image of the *combined* magnetism when projecting or charging with personal magnetism —the two twisted threads in the needle, remember.

Now, to return to the subject of magnetic currents:

The currents of magnetism not only constantly flow around within the limits of the aura, but often push forward toward other persons who attract the attention of the person. In such cases, the aura seems to stretch out toward the other persons, and even to envelop them in its folds. Remember, I am now speaking of the involuntary action of the aura or magnetic currents, not of the conscious and deliberate projection of the currents from the mind to the other mind. There is an almost automatic action of the aura or magnetic currents in the way just stated, when the interest or attention of the person is arouseed by another person.

Of course, if you insist upon the strictist scientific interpretation of this apparently automatic movement of the currents, I must admit that even in such cases the will of the person is the direct cause of the projection. For, it must be remembered, that in the mental acts of interest and attention there is a non- dliberate action of the will—an automatic action, so to speak. The will is called into operation the moment the attention is attracted—in fact, the attention is a positive act of the will. And, consequently, the will sets into motion the magnetic currents in the direction of the object of attention.

So, you will see, when you are conversing with another person, or addressing a number of persons, you are really sending in their direction a series of currents of personal magnetism, the vibrations of which must affect them unless their own vibrations are of a more positive nature. In fact, very many men of the greatest personal force, whose personal magnetism may actually be felt, employ the force in this manner, and make but little use of the "direct flash" methods of immediate concentrated magnetic force, which you will be asked to consider in the suceeding chapters. Their general store of personal magnetism is so great—their personal atmosphere so charged—that mere contact with it produces the result.

But while the above general method of magnetic influence is very effective, provided the individual has learned to sufficiently charge himself, it still remains that the method is that of the shotgun, as compared to that of the rifle, and uses up much power while a smaller amount would suffice. Everything points to the value of a concentrated force, rather than that of the scattered energy. At the last, however, the best method is that which employs both the shotgun and rifle methods—the rifle bullet going right to the mark, surrounded by a cloud of flying shot which completes the work, and renders success certain. So, therefore, when you become interested in the "direct flash" methods in the succeeding chapters, do not lose sight of the important part in personal influence played by the general effect of the magnetism of the aura.

Before I leave this subject, I wish to explain a certain bit of phenomena which has puzzled many students of personal magnetism. I allude to the apparently unconscious use of magnetic power which we so often witness.

For instance, you may be thinking intently of some other person, without any conscious intention of influencing them in any manner, and yet, when you meet the person afterward, or hear from him, you will find that he has been influenced by your magnetic currents, often very markedly so. This is puzzling, when you remember that you made no effort to influence the person by the "direct flash" method, and when you remember that the person was far removed from your personal atmosphere or aura. What is the answer? you ask.

The explanation is this: By your concentrated attention and interest, you have actively (though unconsciously) set the will into motion, and the result is that there has been projected toward the other person a current of your magnetism—a great stretching-out of your personal atmosphere in his direction—and he has been affected by it just as if he had been in your presence. Of course, the other person will not be greatly affected by your currents, unless these happen to be charged with great physical magnetism, and strongly colored by your mental status. But, nevertheless, there will always be some influence exerted, unless, indeed, the other person is more positive, magnetically, than are you, in which case he will not be affected in the least.

So you see, we not only are constantly surrounded by an aura or atmosphere of our magnetic currents, but are also more or less unconsciously sending forth currents of our magnetism into the aura of others, which exert more or less influence upon them. In the same way, the currents of others are constantly reaching our aura, and exerting more or less influence upon us, unless we happen to be more positive than they, in the matter of our vibrations—or (note this), unless we deliberately use an effort of the will in the direction "shutting the door" on these outside vibrations.

CHAPTER XIV.

THE "DIRECT FLASH"

We now approach a phase of the general subject of personal magnetism which is highly important, as well as most interesting to the student, because of its striking and startling features. This phase consists of the deliberate, conscious projection of personal magnetism into the aura of another person, or persons; or into the atmosphere of a crowd of persons. This method has been called the "direct flash," because is resembles the flash of the electric spark, rather than the diffused discharge of a steady current of electricity.

The "direct flash" is the method employed in projecting a positive influence in the direction of others—a mental command backed up by the combined physical and mental magnetism. The method is: (1) The forming in the mind of a direct command, accompanied by a mental picture of the desired action on the part of the other person; (2) the mental gathering of the two combined forces of magnetism into one force; and (3) the deliberate discharge of the "flash" by the will.

You have been fully instructed regarding the first two phases of this "direct flash" method; and you have been given general information which will enable you to comprehend the third phase, i. e., that of the "deliberate discharge of the 'flash' by the will." That is to say, you understand the forming of the mental picture, and the projection of magnetism, in connection with the gathering up of the two forms of magnetism; and you likewise are acquainted with the power and action of the will in the work of projecting magnetism. All you need to complete the instruction regarding the method of using the "direct flash" is a little further instruction regarding the use of the will in projecting this "deliberate discharge." And this further instruction I shall now give you.

The key to the "direct flash" consists in the deliberate action of the will in projecting or "flashing" into the mind of the other person a certain direct statement or command, backed up by all the magnetic forces within you. This comes easily and rapidly as the result of a little practice. And moreover, you may practice in private, standing before your mirror, until you acquire the mental mechanical ease which is necessary.

Let us now begin with some concrete examples, rather than continuing the general consideration. In other words, let us now "get down to brass tacks," in the matter.

Preliminary Exercise. Stand before your mirror, gaze positively and firmly at your own image therein, just as you would gaze toward another person. In fact, you must try to imagine that you are really gazing at another person. Then, send that imaginary person—pictured by your reflected image—the message: *"I am stronger than you!"*

Now, try to get my exact meaning, as I proceed. You must not rest content with merely *thinking* or *saying* the words of the magnetic command above given—you must cultivate and develop an actual *willing* the command, just as you would *will* the raising of your hand, or the clenching of your fist. You will find it necessary to cultivate this power of so willing, for your belief will not at first coordinate with the will. You could not very well will your hand to be lifted, or your fist clenched, unless you actually *believed* that the thing itself were possible. In the same way the little child has to first learn the possibility of using his will, deliberately, in performing physical actions. He first sees others performing certain actions, and the idea gradually dawns upon him that he, too, may do them. Then he begins to use his will, awkwardly at first, in directing the muscles as required. In the same way will you have to develop your ability to use your will deliberately in the direction of this form of personal magnetism. But by a little steady, earnest practice before the mirror, you will soon master the mechanism of the thing—the rest will all be a matter of practice upon persons.

In sending the message, "I am stronger than you," you must accompany the effort of the will (by which you send forth the thought-command) with a strong mental conviction that you *are* stronger (magnetically) than him, and also with the belief that he will be impressed by this fact and will accept your statement. You must get yourself into the mental attitude of *demanding* that he accept your statement, not that you merely request him to do so. In this form of magnetic influence there is no such thing as "requesting"—

it is all a matter of "insistent command"—do
not forget this. When you merely request,
you usually take second magnetic position,
giving to the other person the first place. But
when you command, you take first place,
yourself, and push him into the second. In
practicing before your mirror, remember this,
and endeavor to raise yourself into the first
position. You will know when you have done
this, by the peculiar feeling of superior magnetic strength that you will experience.

After having mastered the above exercise
to your own satisfaction—that is, until you
have thoroughly acquired the feeling of mastery, and magnetic superiority, when you send
forth the flash of command—you may proceed
to the following, which is based upon the
first, and results from it. I mean, that you
are now in a position to practice this second
stage of the exercise before the mirror. You
will feel like beginning to try your power
upon other persons, but you would do better
to wait until you have thoroughly mastered
the mechanism of magnetism before the
mirror.

This second stage of the preliminary mirror exercise, is summed up in the word of

mental magnetic command, which you address
to the imaginary person represented by your
reflected image, viz: "I can command you
to act." This, as you will see by a careful
consideration of the words, is really a tre-
mendously powerful statement, and it will
require a great exercise of your power of
belief, and mental imagery, to get yourself
into the proper mental state, so that the will
may travel easily on its path to enforce the
command. Remember, that in order for the
will to be able to move smoothly over its
channel, so that it may reach the mark, it
is necessary that you clear away any obstacles
that may remain in your own mind. It is
enough for the will to have to fight and break
down the obstacles in the mind of the other
person, without also being called on to combat
and overcome the obstacles in your own mind.
So, you must get yourself in the proper mental state, before you can hope to influence
others.

When you send forth the mental command
to the reflected image, you must concentrate
a tremendous power of meaning in the statement, "I can *command* you to act." The
statement must be accompanied by the full

force of your own conviction and belief that you can so command, and that you will be obeyed. And, in order to do this, you will have to arouse in yourself the full consciousness of your own magnetic force, so that you can fairly *feel* it vibrating in and around you. You will have to re-read these instructions several times before they will become perfectly clear to you. In fact, you will have to begin practicing, and then re-reading them between exercises, before you will get the full meaning. The meaning will gradually unfold into your understanding, as you proceed with your practicing. It is just as if I were giving you directions as to mastering the art of skating—you would not really grasp the full meaning of the instructions until you began actually practicing on the ice—and each time you would refer to the book, you would perceive a new meaning to the words. So it is in the case before us—you will understand the instructions fully only when you begin the actual practice.

Now, after you have gotten to the point in the mirror-practice where you are able to actually *feel* that you have sent forth to the reflected image the command that you are stronger, thereby forcing the other person into the second magnetic place—and also that you can command the other person to act as you will, thereby placing him in the subordinate capacity of action—you may proceed to try upon the reflected image some special commands in the same spirit. Now do not fall into the error of supposing that all this mirror-practice is merely "child's play." If you do, you will be making a great mistake, for it is anything but play or idle pastime. It is the learning of the mechanism of the "direct flash," before you start in to run the machine in earnest. It is like the period of preliminary practice in anything which precedes the actual performance. It is the rehearsal which must precede the play. Do not fail to faithfully perform the rehearsal exercises, before you begin to manifest your magnetism in earnest. You must fully acquaint yourself with your magnetic machine before you begin to run it in earnest.

The preceding practice exercises may be followed by a similar practice of sending forth "flashes" of anything that you may wish to actually send to other persons later on. You may supply these commands for yourself, or you may practice on the following excellent commands, all of which are likely to be used by you in your actual manifestation of personal magnetism. These commands may be varied, of course, to suit your tastes. They must all be delivered before the mirror, in exactly the same manner as I have already stated:

"Look at me!"

"Give me your full attention!"

"Come this way!"

"Go away from me—let me alone!"

"You like me." "You love me!"

"You feel like doing as I wish you to do!"

"You want to please me!"

"You will agree to my proposition!"

"Get out of my way!"

"You are attracted toward me!"

"I fascinate you!"

"I am your MASTER!"

"Come! Be quick, and do as I tell you!"

"You are receptive to my wishes!"

"You are responsive to my will!"

CHAPTER XV.

EXERCISES IN THE "DIRECT FLASH."

And, now, having mastered the preliminary mirror-exercises, you are ready to begin your experiments on real persons. But, here, too, you must crawl before you can walk and run. You must begin with the simpler forms of magnetic influence, before you can accomplish the more complicated or diffcult tasks. But, you have now emerged from the kindergarten stage, and are ready to practice in earnest. If you have faithfully followed the instructions in the mirror-practice, you have mastered the mechanism of magnetic influence, and are ready to "run the machine" in public view. But do not for a moment lose what you have gained in the mirror-exercise. Hold tight and fast to the "technique" you have acquired, and do not for a moment fall into the error that you must now begin all over again. The thing for you to remember, always, is that you are really but carrying the mirror-exercises forward on a higher scale, in a broader field. And you will find some interesting work ahead of you, take my word for it.

First Exercise. I shall now give you an exercise that is almost always given to beginners, by the best teachers of magnetism. It consists of the process of causing a person ahead of you, on the street, to turn around as if he had heard some one call out to him by name. The process is very simple. You have but to walk some little distance behind the other person, on the street, park or other public place. Concentrate your fixed attention on the person, gazing at the lower back part of his head, and sending him first a strong flash of magnetic force, this being followed by the "direct flash" command: "Here you! Turn around!" just as if you were actually calling out aloud to him. You may even whisper the words so softly that no one else can hear them—this may help you to put force into the command, at first, but you will soon outgrow the need of the same. At the time you send the flash command you must actually WILL that the person will turn around in your direction. Put all the magnetic force within you, in this effort.

You will find that in some cases the other person will turn his head almost at once, and look inquiringly behind him in your direction. In the majority of cases, however, he will take a longer time about it. He will be apt to first grow uneasy and restless, and begin by glancing from side to side, as if looking for someone; then he will almost (but not quite) turn his head around; then, finally he will glance backward somewhat furtively and sus-piciousll. No two persons act precisely alike in this respect; and, then, again, the same person will act differently under different conditions. There are certain times at which the conditions seem to be more favorable than at others, for various reasons, as you will discover for yourself.

You will find, in this as well as the following other exercises, that the best results will be obtained while the other person is proceeding idly along, without his attention being directed particularly in any direction.

When the attention is free, the mind is more open to outside influences. When the other person's attention is firmly fixed on anything else, it will be found difficult to influence him to any marked degree. This is the result

of an established rule of psychology, and will
be found to be operative in all cases, as, for
instance, if you call a person when he is pre-
occupied either with deep thought, or else
when his attention is fixed on something in
his surroundings—he will probably not hear
you call him, though under other conditions
he would turn readily. The same rule is, of
course, operative in the case of magnetic
influence.

Second Exercise. When in church, theatre
or other public place, or even in a room full
of company, fix your gaze at the lower back
of the head of some person in the place, and
send him the "direct flash" command:
"Here, you; Turn around and look at me!"
using all the magnetic force within you, and
putting the force of your will back of the command.

You will notice the same peculiar result as
in the preceding exercise, i. e., the fidget-
ing in the seat, the uneasiness and restless-
ness, the final quick turn of the head in your
direction, followed by the confused expression of countenance. In both of these cases,
you should maintain a calm, uninterested
gaze ahead, apparently not noticing the per-

son. It is not well to have persons get the idea that you are experimenting upon them, at any time. There is no power so potent as the silent, reserved power. So keep your own counsel, and do not scatter and weaken your force by talking about it to others—far less by boasting about it. There are certain good psychological and occult reasons for my admonition regarding keeping your own counsel, and not dissipating your energy by talking about it, or revealing it to others. I shall not say more on the subject at this time—but I want you to remember what I have said, *and to heed it.*

Third Exercise. This is a variation of the first exercise, and consists of making the person ahead of you turn to the right or to the left while walking ahead of you. This may follow your exercise of making him turn around. When he approaches another person, send him a flash to move to the right, or to the left, as you will. You may also command a person in like manner when he is approaching you. You will be surprised at your success in this direction, after a little practice. In the case of a very sensitive subject, you can cause him, or her, to zigzag in a comical manner. Do not overdo this, however, or you may defeat your own object, besides being unkind to the sensitive person.

Fourth Exercise. This is a variation of the second exercise, and consists in making the seated person, in front of you, turn and glance to the right, and then to the left, as you will. During the exercise, which may extend over some time, you may obtain some very marked results from the experiment, in some cases. As before, I caution you against going too far with the experiment, lest you be noticed by others, and also, because it is not fair to the subject.

Fifth Exercise. In this experiment, you command the other person to drop his cane, or umbrella, etc., or her fan, handkerchief, etc. In short, you cause the other person to perform some little muscular action under the control of your will.

Sixth Exercise. The above exercise may be varied by sending passing persons various commands, while you are seated at your window, or on your porch, etc. You may put in an interesting hour in sending flashes to the passing crowd, one at a time, of course, and then noting the percentage of successes. You

will find that the percentage will vary; but
the general degree of success should slowly
but steadily increase, on the average. Do
not make the tests too complicated, but send
the flash to perform some very simple motion.
You will be surprised to discover what a
large percent of the persons will glance in
your direction, even though you have not particularly commanded them to do so. This
latter result occurs because of the general
attraction that they will feel toward you,
by reason of the influence of your magnetic
waves.

Seventh Exercise. While I have advised
you to look directly at the other persons, in
sending the flash, this is not absolutely necessary after you have fully acquired the
"mechanism" of the flash. In fact, after
a short time, you will be able to obtain the
result even though your eyes be turned in
another direction. It is not your eye that
influences them, but merely that by gazing
intently you manage to firmly concentrate
your attention and will in their direction.
You may try the experiment of gazing
straight thead of you in a public place, or
on the street, and then flashing the command

to the other person to look at you, and you will find that you will meet with quite a large percentage of success, particularly after you have succeeded with the gazing plan of procedure.

Eighth Exercise. After having mastered the above exercise, you may proceed to a still higher form of magnetic influence, namely, that of influencing the speech of another person. You proceed in this case in the same general manner as in the exercises just given. When a person is speaking to you, you may "put words into his mouth" by a strong mental command, or magnetic flash. Do not try to make him say a whole sentence—at least at first. Rather begin by waiting until he pauses in his speech, and then strongly will a certain word to him—a word that will naturally fit into his sentence—and he will be very apt to repeat it. After a little practice you can make him repeat an absurd word, or to stammer, halt and stutter in his speech, if you so will it. After still more practice, you may succeed in causing him to repeat a whole sentence, or even more, to express the thought you have put into his mind; or to ask some question which you have willed that he should ask.

You will readily see by this time, that a constant practice along these lines, will result in your acquiring the power to will and magnetically influence another person to do many things, in response to your will, and silent command. In fact, a constant development along these lines will make of one a very giant in magnetic power, whose results are proportioned only by the degree of magnetic force of other persons, or the degree of persistent practice and development on his own part.

But I wish to caution you, at this point, against using this power for any unworthy purpose. This caution does not arise from merely a moral motive on my part, but from a knowledge of certain psychic laws which cause a "reaction equaling the action," and which will bring sorry results to you if you violate the rule. So long as you use your new-found power for purely scientific experiments, or legitimate purposes of human association, all very well and good. But never prostitute your power to accomplish unworthy or criminal ends, lest you become involved in a storm of your own raising—or enmeshed in a web of your own weaving.

There are certain psychical laws, as well as physical laws, which must not be broken—and this is one of them. This is particularly true of the case of a person using the power for the purpose of influencing the other sex in an immoral direction. All the old occult writers caution particularly against this practice. So heed the advice, and do the right thing only, with your power.

CHAPTER XVI.

THE POSITIVE AURA.

Now that you have mastered the technique or mechanism of the "direct flash," you are ready to proceed to the actual demonstration or practice thereof in your everyday association and contact with the general public. But, before taking up that phase of the subject, I think it well to ask you to consider the matter of the creation and maintenance of the positive aura. I have purposely postponed the consideration of this phase of the subject, until we reached this particular point in the instruction, because, in order to properly create and maintain the positive aura, it is necessary that one understands the mechanism and technique of the "direct flash," for he will need to manifest the same power in the case of the positive aura. But, now that you have mastered the technique or mechanism of the "direct flash," you are ready to receive the instruction regarding

144

the positive aura, and we may as well proceed to consider it at this very point.

I have already given you instructions regarding the cultivation of a desirable personal atmosphere, or aura, and need not repeat here what I have already said elsewhere. But, a moment's consideration will show you that there will arise certain conditions or occasions in which you will find it very desirable to be able to influence a number of persons en masse—the crowd as a whole—rather than to send the "direct flash" to each of the individuals separately. Of course, the crowd will be influenced by your general personal atmosphere, but you now need something more positive, and more to the point. And the "positive aura" is what you must acquire to satisfy this requirement.

The positive aura is simply the general personal atmosphere, but directly and positively charged by a concentrated effort of the will—the same effort, in fact, as that made in the case of the "direct flash."

Let me illustrate the "positive aura" by means of several stories from real life—the experiences of several students of mine. These personal experiences will give you a

better idea of just what is needed than would
pages of general instruction on the subject.
The little stories are not fiction, remember,
but are "taken from life," and are bits of
human documents from the lives of real people, all of which have come under my personal observation and consideration.

Several years ago, in Paris, I had a student whose real strength of character was
marred by her abnormal self-consciousness,
shyness, timidity, and sensitiveness—in fact,
in the word "sensitiveness" you have the
keynote of this young woman's personality.
She was a young artist of far more than the
average talent, and her charm of manner
rendered her company sought after by a large
circle of friends.

This lady complained to me that she suf-
fered from the actual rudeness, nay, almost
positive brutality, of the crowds of persons
thronging the busy streets of some of the
principal thoroughfares of Paris. She complained that she was jostled here and there,
and pushed rudely aside by the passing
throng. Moreover, she was treated rudely
in the shops, the superficial veneer of polite-
ness of the average Parisian shop-clerk

scarcely concealing the underlying contempt and veiled sneer of these "cheap" satellites of the ubiquitous shop-keepers of this charming city.

My first thought was that the young woman had worked herself up into a state of imaginary wrongs, the result of her highly sensitive organism and shrinking disposition—in short, I thought that she was suffering from a state of morbid self-consciousness, with its frequent accompaniment of imaginary persecution, etc. So I determined to test out the matter, and ascertain for myself just how much truth was in the case.

Making a slight change in my personal appearance, by means of a simple disguise once taught me by another of my students, a celebrated detective of Paris, I followed the young lady for several hours when she was on a shopping expedition. Much to my surprise, and, I may add, much to my indignation, I found that all that she had told me was correct. I could scarcely control myself at times, and more than once felt like chastising some rude fellow with my cane, so brutal was the conduct of certain individuals calling themselves "men."

There is a certain class of Parisian men, well-dressed and with a veneer of polish, but boors and curs at heart. These men seem to take a special delight in jostling young women, almost pushing them off the sidewalks, at times, and in other ways earning a good canning at the hands of real gentlemen. Well, these curs seemed attracted to this sweet young girl, just as flies are drawn to a bit of sugar. They exceeded themselves in their display of rudeness and cowardly insolence, and all the while the girl was free from any outward appearance that would attract such curs naturally. I saw at once that there was some inner cause operating.

Moreover, I noticed that the young woman was also pushed aside rudely by hurrying business persons, who never glanced in her direction, but who thrust her aside as if she were an inanimate thing instead of a person. Again I found an inner cause. In the same way I found that she was treated exactly in the way she had complained of in the shops, by the clerks and shop-men, although she was a liberal customer, easily suited, and giving but little trouble. Here again, the inner trouble was apparent.

I went home and carefully diagnosed the case, and laid down a course or treatment. I sent for the young woman and told her just what the trouble was. I told her that her trouble was a case of "ingrown sensitiveness, and overgrown modesty"—in short, that she had surrounded herself with an aura of self-depreciation and morbid sensitiveness. This aura practically invited persons to "pick on" her, to crowd her to the wall, to push her in the gutter, and to generally slight, snub and covertly insult her in the shops. Her aura was not only negative, but actually attractively negative—that is to say, so negative that it actually attracted more positive natures in the direction of imposing on her weakness. (This is far from being unusual —it is a rule of the psychic as well as of the physical world, among animals as well as among men.)

I immediately began teaching this lady the technique of the "direct flash" before the mirror (exactly as I have taught you), her flashes being invariably along the lines of positivity and strength. She would flash out "I am positive—far more positive than the crowd around me," "Get out of my way,

or I will walk over you;" "Clear the path for
me, you vermin," and other exaggerated
demands intended for the street crowds. In
the same way she would flash out the command to the shop-people: "Come, now, I demand respectful attention;" "Lively, now,
attend to my wants;" "I am a princess of
the blood, bow to me, you underlings," etc.
You will note that I purposely exaggerated
the mental demands and flashes, because she
needed an exaggerated positive mental attitude in order to overcome her natural and
acquired handicap. In a short time she had
acquired the technique perfectly and had
developed a mental attitude and general personal atmosphere of a princess. Then she
proceeded to "try it on the crowd," by means
of the "positive aura."

The result was marvelous. From the moment her feet touched the sidewalk, her progress was that of a princess, persons instinctively moved out of her way, some even
slightly bowing as they did so. The rowdy
gentlemen(?) moved far away from her. And
in the shops the queen of England could have
received no more humble service or careful
attention. The cure was complete, and has

remained so. The young lady has long since laid aside the "Princess Royal" manner, and now simply maintains an aura of positive self-respect and self-confidence, and a demand that she be accorded the proper consideration.

Another case is that of a young student of mine—and American, the son of a prominent business man. This young man was well educated, polished, and moreover, possessed of all the requisites of a successful salesman, except that of inspiring a feeling of friendship on the part of those with whom he came in contact. He was called upon to approach prominent business men in connection with his work for his father, and while he was able to present his arguments logically and forcibly, he was nevertheless handicapped by the fact that he *repelled* friendship, rather than invited it. In desperation, he made the trip across the Atlantic to consult me, and to beg a cure for his serious psychic trouble.

His cure was very easy. I simply put him through a course of the mirror exercises in the "direct flash," until he had mastered the technique; and then had him saturate his mind with the mental image and idea of:

"You like me—you like me very much;" "You feel attracted toward me;" "You are my friend, and wish to show your friendship for me," etc., etc., etc. All these ideas were but variations of, and improvements upon, the simple idea of "You like me!"

Well, this young man began to radiate such an atmosphere of likeability, friendship, etc., that he made friends right and left, even without trying—it was in the air around him, it seemed. His old trouble disappeared like magic—he was made over into a new man. And, yet it was all very simple, you see. Mere child's play, when one has the secret as *you* now have. The young man insisted upon presenting me with his checque for $1,000, although I had charged him but one-tenth of that amount, for my time and trouble.

I could go into this vein, reciting case after case coming under my own experience, but I think that the two cases I have mentioned will give you the general idea of what I am trying to teach you, without my taking up more time and space at this point. The rule is general—it is for you to apply it to the particular requirements of your own case.

Find out your weak spots of personal atmosphere, and then proceed to build up the opposite qualities of mind and character. Find out your negative points of attraction, and then proceed to build of their opposite positive qualities, just as the two students, just mentioned, did with such marked success. Read over carefully this chapter again, and again, until you get the joint fixed in your mind. The rest is merely a matter of practice

CHAPTER XVII.

THE DIRECT COMMAND.

Having by this time acquired the technique of the "direct flash," by your mirror-practice; and having, also, mastered the art of cultivating the positive aura, you should be able to manifest what is known as "the direct command," without much additional instruction.

By "the direct command" is meant the flashing of a direct command or demand to the mind of another person, backed up by the concentrated power of both your mental and physical magnetism. Do you see now why I have first taught you to acquire the technique by means of the mirror-practice, and have then next taught you how to generate and maintain the positive aura? Certainly, you have seen the point! A moment's thought will show you that the "direct command" is really a combination of the methods of the mirror-practice, and that of the posi-

tive aura. The mirror-practice taught you the technique, and the practice afforded by the positive aura methods have served to give you ease, self-confidence, and an almost instinctive use of your magnetic powers in the direction of influencing other persons. You will also see the part played in your development by the special exercises in the direct flash, which I gave you in a preceding chapter. You now begin to see why I have led you to the present point by degrees, do you not?

The "direct command" is really a high form of the "direct flash," and is the method whereby the latter may be used to the highest degree of effectiveness.

In the "direct command" you flash your command to the mind of the other person, mentally, of course, but in exactly the same way that you would make an actual command by spoken words, if the conditions admitted of the same. You form the words of the command in your mind, carrying with it as strong a mental picture as you can create, and then mentally flash the command to the other person with as much magnetic force as you can muster.

You will find it an aid to effectiveness, in the case of a contemplated demand upon some particular person, for a certain thing, to practice it before the mirror, using your own image as a "target"—just as you did in the exercise previously given you. You will find that a rehearsal of this kind will tend to increase your power at the time of the actual manifestation or command.

It is impossible to give you specific instruction for the carrying out of this program in special cases, for each person will have his or her own special requirements, the same depending upon the special circumstances of the case. All that I can do is to give you the general directions, and then trust that you will have sufficient ingenuity to apply these general rules to your own particular cases and requirements. The general rules I have already given you. Perhaps I can illustrate the application of the same by citing a few cases which have actually come under my own observance and experience.

One of the most interesting cases of the kind that I have ever met with, was that of a professor in one of the American universities. This man, a specialist in his particular line of scientific research, and a thorough master of his own particular subject, commanded a large audience of readers of his books and magazine articles, but, at the same time was almost a failure in his class work, owing to his inability to gain and hold the attention of his students. He came to me, in Paris, and explained his trouble. I gave him my short course in mental influence, etc., and drilled him well along the lines laid down in this book. I made him practice before an imaginary roomful of students, sending them a strong direct command of "Give me your full attention!" "Steady, now, your attention—your full and complete attention to my words!" and "That's right, you are giving me your full attention—now hold it firmly fixed on me!" and a similar stock of direct commands. These commands were directed first to the "bell-wethers" of the class—those natural leaders who are to be found in each class, and then scattered among the class at large. The professor told me that, after a number of these imaginary class-room scenes, he could actually see the class before him, each face being distinct and plain, and that he could almost see the flash of his command reaching them.

When I thought that he had mastered the general principles, and acquired the technique, I dismissed him, and he returned at once to the university in America. I received several letters from him during the following year, and he testified to the complete success of the plan when put into actual effect. From the first day of his return he obtained and held the attention of his class, and to-day he is one of the best personal instructors in his university, or elsewhere for that matter. In this case he applied the direct command to special individuals of the class, but the principle was the same as in the case of a single special individual, and differed from the positive aura method.

Another case was that of a promoter, now of international reputation, who formerly was unable to "close" many of his plans, owing to a lack of something in his mental makeup, he thought. He could evolve plans which attracted the attention of prominent men and others, and he could also manage to fascinate them by his general talk regarding his enterprises. But he found it most difficult to induce them to take the final step of "coming in," or signing the contract, or entering the subscription, as the case might be.

I labored with this man, experiencing much trouble in overcoming his fixed and stubborn idea that there was "something wrong" with his mental makeup. Finally, after a long period of careful drilling before an imaginary "prospect" (this term being applied to prospective customers) he began to *feel* that he had the missing element, after all. From that moment he was filled with new courage, and threw new life and energy into the exercises. So powerfully magnetic was this man, and so high a degree of concentrated force did he generate, that I could actually *feel* the force of his power while present in the room directing the exercises. I actually, myself, felt like subscribing to some of his stock, and am sure that had he approached me on the subject it would have required the exercise of my full power of self-protection and resistance to have overcome his magnetism.

When this man finished his instruction at my hands, he at once plunged into the floating of a new great enterprise, and carried same to a most successful conclusion. He "closed" nearly every "prospect" that he approached, and soon dropped all the smaller "prospects," and devoted his entire attention to

the "large fish." I do not feel at liberty to
state here the axact words of the "direct
command" used by him, for he paid me a
large fee for my own services, and the secret
should be his own, under the circumstances
—but this I will say, that his direct command was a straight out from the shoulder
mental DEMAND upon the "prospect" to
"come in."

Another interesting case was that of a now
well-known actress, who lacked "fascination." She was a magnificent actress, of fine
presence and a thorough knowledge of her
art, but for some reason her acting seemed
to lack soul. She came to me to learn how to
influence her audience by personal magnetism, but I saw at once that her art, if fully
exercised, would be sufficient to carry her
audiences with her. Her trouble lay in the
fact that there was a certain "fascination"
lacking. I set her to work, training her so
that she would actually fascinate the actors
playing with her(and an air of reality would
be thus created. She progressed rapidly, so
quick were her perceptions. When she left
me she was able to throw such a degree of
fascination into her voice and manner, that
the actor playing with her would be **fairly**

swept off his feet; the result being that the audience would catch the same by a kind of mental contagion. She simply hurled mental direct commands at the actors, while reciting her lines, and while approaching them. Her success is now assured, but I cannot resist the temptation of mentioning that she has had the greatest trouble with her "leading man" in her companies—they all insist and persist in falling in love with her, and she has had to change them frequently to get rid of their unwelcome attentions, for her heart is "taken" elsewhere.

I feel that I am justified in calling the attention to another case—that of a leading statesman who took my instructions by means of a series of letters, several years ago. This man wanted MASTERY. He got it. I gave him the cue, and keynote, and he did the rest. So masterful did he become, by the employment of my suggested direct commands, that he dominated all who came near him. In fact he carried the thing a little too far—he grew to be regarded as dangerous and tyranica. and powerful interests conspired against him. He is in temporary retirement at this time—but he is really but biding his time. It is impossible to remain in this man's presence for any time—particularly if his attention is directed toward you—without acknowledging him to be a MASTER.

I now ask you to refer to the last pages of the chapter on the "direct flash." You will find there a number of sentences given as practices before the mirror. Study over these sentences carefully, and you will find therein a strong hint of the idea which you should weave into your own direct commands. All of these sentences have been effectively employed by students of mind, under my direction, in actual practice—and all of them have the germ of success in them. You may use them singly, in combination, or as a general pattern around which you may weave your own ideas. Practice each of them, until you catch the spirit, and you will then have no trouble in creating your own commands in the most approved style. You will notice the DIRECTNESS and POSITIVENESS of each of these commands—these are the two essential qualities to be observed and used in this work of the direct command. Put all your magnetic force behind them, and flash them out right to the point—squarely into the mentality of the persons whom you wish to influence.

CHAPTER XVIII.

THE MAGNETIC DUEL.

The laws of personal magnetism are in accord with the other laws of nature in recognizing the universal fact that there are various degrees of power, and that, all else being equal, the stronger power will prevail over the weaker. But, it is likwise true that the individual, by a superior knowledge of the art of science of defense and offense, may often triumph over a superior degree of strength in the other person. This fact is as true of personal magnetism as it is of physical strength. The skilled magnetic individual may overcome his stronger adversary, just as the skilled boxer may overcome a stronger man, or a skilled fencer may disarm and defeat a much stronger opponent.

The conflict between the opposing magnetism of individuals is to be seen on all hands everyday. In fact, it has been well said that two persons never meet but that there is at least a preliminary trial of magnetic strength At any rate, no two persons ever meet, whose interests are in the least opposed, but that there occurs a little tilt of magnetic strength —sometimes a quite strenuous test, in fact. And in these tests there always is one trium· phant and one defeated. It is true that the circumstances of the case sometimes affect the result, and the defeated to-day may be the victor to-morrow, but the fact remains, that for the time being, at least, there is always one on top and the other underneath at the finish of the magnetic duel, be it slight or serious. One has but to recall incidents in his own experience to recognize this fact.

Oliver Wendell Holmes recognized this magnetic duel, in one of his books, when he speaks of "that deadly Indian hug in which men wrestle with their eyes, over in five seconds, but which breaks one of their two backs, and is good for three score years and ten, one trial enough—settles the whole matter—just as when two feathered songsters of the barnyard, game and dunghill, come together. After a jump or two, and a few sharp kicks, there is an end of it; and it is 'After you, monsieur' with the beaten party in all the social relations for all the rest of his days."

Dr. Fothergill, a well-known English physician, now deceased, once wrote a little book upon the subject of the will. The good doctor was a close student of personal magnetism, although he did not choose to use the term itself in his writings, because of the narrow code of professional ethics then imposed upon the medical profession in Great Britian. I have personal reasons, however, for asserting that the doctor was an advanced student of personal magnetism, in theory and practice. I therefore take great pleasure in quoting from him on the particular subject now before us, as follows:

"The conflict of will, the power to command others, has been spoken of frequently. Yet what is this will-power which influences others? What is it that makes us accept, and adopt too, the advice of one person, while precisely the same advice from another has been respected? Is it the weight or force of will which insensibly influences us; the force of will behind the advice? That is what it is! The person who thus forces his or her adivce upon us has no more power to enforce it than others; but all the same we do as requested. We accept from one. what we reject from another. One person says of something contemplated, 'Oh, but you must not,' yet we do it all the same, though that person may be in a position to make us regret the rejection of that counsel. Another person says, 'Oh, but you mustn't,' and we desist, though we may, if so disposed, set this latter person's opinion at defiance with impunity. It is not the fear of consequences, nor of giving offense, which determines the adoption of the latter person's advice, while it has been rejected when given by the first. It depends upon the character or will-power of the individual advising whether we accept the advice, or reject it. This character often depends little, if at all, in some cases, upon the intellect, or even on the moral qualities, the goodness or badness, of the individual. It is itself an imponderable something; yet it carries weight with it. * * * There may be abler men, cleverer men; but it is the one possessed of will who rises to the surface at these times—the one who can by some subtle power make other men obey him. * * * The will-struggle goes on universally. In the young aristocrat, who gets his tailor to make another advance in defiance of his conviction that he will never get his money back. It goes on between lawyer and client; betwixt doctor and patient; between banker and borrower; betwixt buyer and seller. It is not tact which enables the person behind the counter to induce customers to buy what they did not intend to buy, and which when bought, gives them no satisfaction, though it is linked therewith for the effort to be successful. Whenever two persons meet in business, or in any other relation in life, up to love-making, there is this will-fight going on, commonly enough without any consciousness of the struggle. There is a dim consciousness of the result, but none of the processes. It often takes years of the intimacy of married life to find out with whom of the pair the mastery really lies. Often the far stronger character, to all appearances, has to yield; it is this will-element which underlies the statement: 'The race is not always to the swift, nor the battle to the strong.' In 'Middlemarch' we find in Lydgate a grand aggregation of qualities, yet shallow, hard, selfish Rosamond masters him thoroughly in the end. He was not deficient in will-power, possessed more than an average share of character; but in the fight he went down at last under the onslaught of the intense, stubborn will of his narrow-minded spouse. Their will-contest was the collision of a large, warm-nature, like a capable human hand, with a hard, narrow, selfish nature, like a steel button; the hand only bruised itself while the button remained unaffected."

If you will substitute the term "magnetic force," for "will," "will-power," etc., in the good doctor's words, you will see how perfectly he was in accord with the teachings contained in this book.

The student who has carefully studied the foregoing pages will have acquired sufficient knowledge of the theory and practice, the method and the technique, of personal magnetism, to be able to carry himself or herself through a "magnetic duel" with credit to himself or herself, and credit to myself, the teacher. But remember, that there is as much in adroitness, and skill, as there is in mere strength of magnetism. Carry in mind the tactics of the good boxer, or good fencer—try to reproduce (in the magnetic duel) the guards, feints, the unexpected stroke, the rushes, the overpowering stroke, etc. It will not hurt you to purposely engage in some of these conflicts, as good practice preparing for the day of a real test of power on some important point. Assert your will a little, and strive to have your own way in small matters, particularly if you are opposed therein by others. The skill and practice, together with the self-confidence you will gain will prove useful to you in the hour of need.

In addition to the general and special instruction regarding the use of positive magnetism in relation to other persons, I now offer for your consideration the following special "flashes," for use on special occasions, especially in cases of the "magnetic duel." You will find these flashes of great use to you on such occasions, particularly (as is generally the case) where the opponent does not know the secret of his own natural power of magnetism, and is not versed in the art and science of using it. Study over these carefully—-for they are valuable, and represent the result of years of experience and practice. Here follows the list just spoken of:

"My magnetism is stronger than yours— it is overpowering you."

"My magnetism is beating down your guard—you are weakening."

"I am more positive than you—you are negative and are beginning to retreat and give in to me."

"You are beginning to feel afraid of me, afraid, afraid, afraid of me."

"Retreat, retreat, retreat, I tell you—I am forcing you backward."

"I am scattering your forces—I am dissipating your energy—I am breaking your magnetism to bits, by the power of my own force."

"I am standing on the solid rock of power—your feet are on sand, and are slipping way from you."

"GET OUT OF MY WAY—I COMMAND YOU TO GET OUT!"

"I am crowding you back, off your feet; move back, I tell you—BACK, out of my way, I tell you!"

You may get the spirit of the above by carefully reading them, repeating them to your image in the mirror, throwing full force into the words, and the expression into your eyes. Then you will be able to flash them out to others when the occasion arises, with ease,

power and effect. You need not be bound by
the precise words that I have given you, providing yₑu catch the spirit behind them. You
may use your own words—the very words
that you would like to actually utter to the
other person, if you prefer it. The thing to
do is to get the feeling and meaning into his
mind.

In a succeeding chapter, entitled "Magnetic Self-Defence," you will find full instruction for defensive flashes, and "guards,"
which are to be used in connection with the
above offensive ones, in the magnetic duel.
Beat the opponent off by neutralizing his
magnetism, according to the advice given in
the next chapter, and then plunge in your
own mental weapons of attack.

The following constitutes a broad-sword
mental weapon, which may often be used with
the greatest effect:

"I am pouring into you a strong concentrated current of magnetic power, which is
overpowering you and conquering you, and
bending you to my will. My magnetism is
far stronger than is yours, and I know how to
use it to better advantage than do you. I am
overpowering you—I am conquering you—I

am bending you to my will. I am MASTER-ING you, steadily and completely. I shall command you to do as I will. You MUST do it, and do it now. Surrender, I tell you—surrender now—SURRENDER to me at once. You MUST, and you SHALL. I am breaking down your resistance. You are giving up—SURRENDER   NOW—SURRENDER   AT ONCE."

CHAPTER XIX.

CORPOREAL MAGNETISM

Before concluding my instruction regarding the subject of the projection of personal magnetism, I wish to have a few words with you on the subject of what may be called "corporeal" magnetism. By "corporeal" is meant "pertaining to the body." I use the term "corporeal magnetism" to indicate and designate the conveyal of personal magnetism by means of physical contact, as, for instance, by the touch of the hands, lips, etc.

It may be objected to that this term is needless, inasmuch as I have already considered the phase of physical magnetism, or nerve-force, in connection with the general subject of personal magnetism. But, I answer, by "corporeal magnetism" I mean something different from mere physical magnetism, or nerve-force. The new term is far more inclusive, for, by "corporeal magnetism" I mean the projection of the combined personal magnetism (physical and mental) to the other person, over the channels of the nervous system of both persons, instead of through the ether as in the case of the ordinary projection of personal magnetism.

Note this distinction: Under the head of physical magnetism, I explained to you how magnetic healing treatments might be given by the use of the hands, the physical magnetism passing over the nervous system of the healer, making the leap between the finger-tips and the body of the other person. But, in "corporeal magnetism" not only the physical magnetism or nerve-force, is so projected to the other person, *but at the same time is also projected the mental magnetism.* In short, the entire process of the projection of combined personal magnetism is performed, but the magnetism flows along physical channels, instead of across the ether, to reach the other person. I trust that you clearly perceive this distinction, before we proceed further.

That there exists this phase of personal magnetism, called "corporeal magnetism" cannot be doubted by the careful investigator. On all sides we may see evidence of the phenomena of this phase of personal magnetism. In the hand-shake of the person is often conveyed the strongest kind of personal magnetism—in the touch of the hand is often found the strongest kind of emotional vibrations. In the kiss, and the contact of the cheek, are often to be found the most active form of emotional vibrations, as almost everyone knows. In short, by bodily contact there may often be conveyed the most dangerous forms of sexual magnetism—and other forms of magnetism.

I do not intend to say much regarding sexual magnetism in this book, but I would not be doing justice to my students if I failed to at least mention some plain facts, in passing. I need scarcely remind my students of the powerful sexual emotions often aroused by a kiss, or touch of the cheek, or even the "holding of hands"—this knowledge is common to the race, although few understand the real nature of the phenomena. Enough for me to say that the libertine generally realizes full well the powerful vibrations which may be conveyed in this manner, although he does not understand the scientific facts of the case —he has the practice well defined in his mind, although he does not understand the theory.

Young persons, especially young women, should be taught the danger of this form of magnetism, and should avoid allowing the physical contact which makes the same active. The "holding hands," the thoughtless kiss, pressure of the cheek, embrace, or close physical contact, all afford and furnish a "direct line" for the passage of this form of magnetism, i. e., the sexual magnetism conveyed through corporeal channels. The unprincipled person, of strong passions, soon learns that by close physical contact he may often convey his emotional vibration to the young woman, and thus arouse reciprocal vibrations which may sweep her off her feet, and into his arms—often to her utter ruin and disgrace. This is not a pleasant subject, but I feel that I would not be true to my students if I failed to point out this dangerous force, and to caution them to guard against the employment of the same against them.

Leaving this phase of the subject, I now wish to call the attention of my students to the use of corporeal magnetism in the ordinary use of the hands, as in shaking hands, etc. Here is a subject worthy of the closest attention on your part.

Strongly magnetic men, and those who have studied this subject, frequently employ this method of projecting personal magnetism in making their preliminary moves in the direction of influencing other persons by personal magnetism. Who has not experienced the magnetic hand-shake of individuals of this kind? And, on the other hand, who has not been conscious of the feeling of repulsion inspired by the cold, clammy, snake-like hand-shake of other types of persons?

You have also probably noticed that many men whose business it is to influence you in any direction, such as politicians, preachers, promoters, salesmen, etc., have a habit of placing their hands upon your shoulders, during the conversation—or laying their hand lightly on your arm while speaking to you— in some cases, giving you a final pat on the back as they urge you to "sign right here, and close the thing up." Have you realized that this is a form of corporeal magnetism, and that the result is often very effective? Look out for these fellows in the future, and neutralize their magnetism according to the rules given in the next chapter of this book. If you choose to employ these methods yourself—well, that is your own business, and a matter for yourself to decide. It is a very strong method of conveying corporeal magnetism, I assure you.

In shaking hands with any person whom you may wish to influence, you should throw into the clasp the strongest possible kind of personal magnetism, physical and mental, according to the rules already given you in this book. Give the person the direct command at the moment of the clasp, throwing it into him by means of the nerves of the hand and fingers. (A little practice, in the direction of shaking hands with yourself will be of great aid to you in this matter). Send him a mental message just as you would if you were merely looking at him.

When you meet a person with whom you are acquainted, the hand-clasp is the natural thing, and it gives you a splendid opportunity to get in a powerful preliminary flash of personal magnetism, accompanied by the strongest possible direct command. When this is performed properly, it will serve to get the other person in exactly the right psychic conditions to receive your further direct commands, and to yield more readily to your magnetism. It is your "advance guard" preparing the way for the grand charge upon the breast-works of the enemy. Use it well and half the battle will be won at one stroke.

Always be hearty in your hand-clasp—not rough or too strenuous, for no one likes to have his hand tightly squeezed or bruised—always remember the word "hearty" in this connection. Beware of the lifeless handshake—throw feeling into it, and make it be alive and vital. Shake hands as if the other person meant something to you, and hold on to his hand for a moment, and then let go as if with reluctance. Seek out some strongly magnetic person, used to meeting people—some successful politician, for instance—and let him shake hands with you. Notice how much interest and feeling he puts into his clasp—and then take notes from his methods. A good magnetic preacher, meeting his flock at the church door as they pass out, also will give you a good example. Study them and "catch the motion."

When shaking hands with a person who you wish to influence, you should throw into the hand-clasp the direct command which you wish to impress upon him. If you wish him,

or her, to like you, your direct command
should be along those lines, for instance, a
strong "You LIKE me!" If you wish to assert your positivity over his power, you
should get to work at once with a very strong
positive "I am *stronger* than *you.*" or "I am
far more POSITIVE than you!" or some
other statement of the same general kind,
such as I have given you in the preceding
chapters. In fact, you may use any or all of
the statements previously given you, in this
form as well as in the ordinary phases of the
direct command.

In concluding this chapter, I wish to call
your attention to a phase of the phenomena
of corporeal magnetism which is often overlooked by teachers of the subject. I allude to
that form of magnetism which is projected by
mere "nearness" of the bodies of persons,
even though direct contact may not be had.
Good salesmen and others often know this
from their own experience, although not understanding the real cause. They know that
by sitting near to the customer, they can get
a better magnetic effect than if compelled to
sit at a little distance. The result of the
"heart to heart" talk often results from this

nearness. In the same way, the gestures of
the hands of a speaker, coming in close contact to other persons, often serves to convey
the magnetism to them, although no actual
contact is had.

The hands, particularly, are very effective
instruments for the conveyal of corporeal
magnetism, for the nerves of the fingers are
very sensitive, and readily convey and project the magnetism with great concentrated
force. The use of the fingers of the mesmerist
is but one example of this fact. You will also
notice that the majority of effective orators
and speakers have a way of making passes
and waves at their audiences. The good
solicitor or promoter usually employs his
hands in this way. Remember, I do not say
that these people are always conscious of the
facts behind their gestures—they often are
ignorant of the same, and use their hands instinctively, having acquired the movements
through habit. But the facts remain, and
those who learn the secret of the force and
its employment, and thereafter use it consciously and deliberately, are placed at a
great advantage over others who do not possess this knowledge. And, mark my words,

there **are thousands** of the world's **greatest** men **who** have learned this secret, **taken** lessons in its use, and are now employing it actively. You may now join their ranks, if **you care to do so.**

CHAPTER XX.

MAGNETIC SELF-DEFENCE.

And, now, having made you acquainted with the various forms of the manifestation, projection and use of personal magnetism—having taught you not only the theory, but also the practice; not only how to acquire the technique, but also how to effectively employ the same—I will conclude by calling your attention to the defensive side of the question. In boxing or fencing, you have not mastered the art fully until you are able not only to attack but also how to defend—not only the art of aggressive action, but also the science of defensive action. And, so it is in the case of personal magnetism, you must not only know how to use the force in the form of projection, but you must also know how to defend yourself against the projection of the force by others.

It is true that the careful and diligent student of these lessons will gradually develop such a power within himself that he

183

will scarcely ever meet individuals **more** powerful than himself. But, still, there **are** always the very strong individuals to be reckoned with, and I want you to possess the secret of dispersing and dissipating the magnetism of such persons, so far as effect on yourself is concerned, by the methods known to all advanced students and practitioners of personal magnetism.

This defensive science is far more simple than you would think at first, although to be effective in the same you must first have learned how to project effectively. I may sum it up in a few words—heed them carefully. The secret is this: *In defending oneself against magnetic projection in any or all of its forms, you have but to project toward the other person a strong DENIAL of his power to influence, affect, or master you.* That is the whole thing in a nutshell. Now for the details.

But, right here, I want to remind you of a very important fact, and that is in this *denial* you do not really destroy or lessen the power of the other person, in general. You only neutralize his magnetism so far as it affects yourself, or those whom you wish to protect.

In other words, instead of destroying his weapons, you merely turn them aside, and cause them to glance off, leaving you, and yours, harmless. To use a familiar illustration from the field of electricity, *you render yourself a non-conductor,* and the force glances off you without affecting you in the slightest. Remember this illustration, and you will have the idea firmly fixed in your mind.

You may render yourself immune not only from the direct flash, and direct demand or command, of others, no matter how strong they may be; but also from the general contagion of the mental atmosphere or auras of others. By proper concentrated effort, along these lines, you may render yourself absolutely immune from the force of the personal magnetism of others, if you so desire. Or, if you prefer, you may shut out only certain individuals from your field, and allow the beneficial magnetism of others to enter it. In truth, you are your own MASTER, if you but exert your power.

As to the methods to be employed, you have but to use those you have already learned in these lessons, by merely changing the mental attitude and statement or command. For instance instead of projecting the direct command that you are stronger than the other person, and can therefore influence him; you have but to calmly DENY his power over you, and defy him to affect you in the slightest. As a matter of fact that mental attitude is far less strenuous than the aggressive form of magnetic projection. It requires merely the interposition of your magnetic shield of defence, and his power will glance off without affecting you, even though he be most strenuously projecting it. There is of course the other plan of fighting aggressive magnetism with aggressive magnetism—this is the real magnetic duel in its plain form, and may be used when desired. But if you merely wish to repel the aggression of others, you have but to use the defensive plan of the DENIAL, as I have just told you.

In forming the mental statement which occompanies all forms of the use of mental magnetism, as you have seen, you merely express (mentally) in a few, strong positive words, the idea you wish to reach the other person's mind. Well, so it is in the case of magnetic self-defence. You simply mentally state in a

few strong words that you deny the power of the other person. You will find, as you experiment, that in the very words "I DENY," there is a mighty dynamic power of defence. It is the mental idea back of these words, which, figuratively wipes out of existence the other person's magnetism, at least so far as you, yourself, are concerned. It is the great SHIELD OF DEFENCE. Let the full meaning of the word "DENY" enter into your mind—you will find it contains a new meaning and strength, when considered in this connection.

Now, right at this point, before proceeding further, I ask you to turn back over the leaves of the preceding lessons, and make note of the numerous statements given to accompany the positive aura, the direct flash, the direct command, etc. Then form in your own mind the denial of these statements (if they are projected by another person), and you will find that you possess instinctively the power to frame such statements of denial, easily. Practice a little, imagining that another person is hurling these flashes or commands at you, and that you are interposing **the shield** of denial in each case. You will be surprised, and delighted, to realize how easily you can repel the strongest of these assaults. You may then begin to practice by throwing yourself into the presence and company of the strongest magnetic persons you know, and then see how easily you can repel their power—and how free, calm and serene you now feel in their presence.

There are two things to be remembered in this connection—I have already told you them, but it is well to repeat them in order to fix them firmly in your mind. I ask you to consider them in the following paragraphs.

In the first place, as I have told you, this defensive process merely enables you to throw off and render yourself immune from the aggressive magnetism of others—it does not enable you to master them or to compel them to do your bidding. In order to accomplish this latter, you must not only beat down the guard of the other person; protect yourself at the same time; and then carry the day by a direct magnetic assault upon him. You can do these things if he fights you with the weapons of aggressive magnetism only, but if he DENY your power, he is immune, and you cannot affect him; just as if you

DENY his power, you are immune—in case both DENY, then the battle is drawn, and neither win. The Denial is not a weapon of aggressiveness—it is merely the shield of defence. Remember this! Of course if you use both shield and sword, you will have a double advantage, providing he does not also use the shield. For if you can repel his magnetism, and at the same time use your own—then he is at your mercy. But if he knows enough to also use his shield—then the battle will be drawn, and neither will win a decided victory. Do you catch the idea? Think over it until it is plain to you.

The second point I wish to impress upon you, in this connection, is the fact, already stated by me, that you do not actually *destroy* or *weaken* the other person's magnetism, by the use of the shield of denial. His magnetism remains just as strong, and just as much in evidence, as if you did not use the shield—the only difference being that by using it you render his weapons powerless against you, or those you may wish to protect; and thus create an immunity for yourself, and your proteges, by interposing the shield of defense. But you do not impair the power of the other person against others whom you do not directly shelter behind your shield. Do you get this point? Think over it until you get it clearly.

When you repel the magnetism of one of the persons who have been using it without knowing the nature of his power (and there are many who so use it—the majority of persons, in fact) you will be amused to see how "broken up" such a person becomes. He will become bewildered at his failure to influence and affect you, and will often become embarrassed and, in some cases, actually entangled in the currents of his own magnetism. It may even happen (it often does, really) that such a person will become so confused by his apparent loss of power, that he will lose his assurance and consequently his ability to attack. In such cases, he becomes an easy subject for a magnetic rush or broadside on your own part, which will quickly drive him into a disastrous retreat. Of course, if he has a scientific knowledge of the subject, he will not be so taken off guard, but, recognizing your knowledge and power, he will pass it off with a smile, and relinquish the attack.

And, now, good student, we part company

for the present. I am glad to have had the
honor of giving you this instruction, in these
lessons, and I trust that you will so conduct
yourself that you will be a creditable pupil
of mine, and do me honor by your accomplish-
ments and attainments. I have supplied you
with the weapons of both aggressive and also
of defensive personal magnetism, and have
taught you how to employ both of them so as
to get the best results. It is now "up to you"
to make the best use of these weapons, according to the rule and principles which I have
laid down for your guidance.

In parting, I wish to again impress two important rules upon you, and these are:

(1) Practice, practice, practice, until you
have every detail of the instruction so well
learned, and so fixed by habit, that you can
and will use them instinctively, just as you
now walk, or breathe, or speak.

(2) Keep your own secrets, and do not
dissipate and scatter your influence by hint-
ing of your secrets of your power over others.
There are many good reasons for this rule—
some reasons that do not appear on the surface, by-the-way.

CHAPTER XXI.

THE POWER OF CONTROLLING OTHERS.

Some special exercises, every one of which is
of great value. They will make you
stronger in mind, will, nerves, and
health generally.

Before proceeding with the lesson, I wish
to caution you never to use your power to
gain something you are not entitled to. You
have a perfect right, however, to us all the
natural forces to gain success. Some may
think that we have no right to control others.
In all my travels I have never met a person
of a strong magnetic personality who was not
honest and true. It is a well known law that
no one will gain the power to control others
until he is able to control himself. This is
very necessary, as otherwise those possessing a strong power would be using this power
to control the opposite sex, and would thus
become entangled in many love affairs.
Therefore, you will have to develop your

character, and learn how to control yourself before you can expect to control others.

Many students who have taken my correspondence course have written to me, stating that after simply reading this lesson through, they have noticed a wonderful change. Some of the statements made in this lesson may sound impossible to you, but I know they are true, and if you will follow the rules given, you will be irristibly led onward and upward and be filled with a firm determination to win.

The pupil of the eye indicates the magnetic condition. The eyes play a very important part in Personal Magnetism. When you look at a person you see some part of the ball of the iris and the pupil. This ball is supposed to be white, but it is veined, and tinted with a delicate color which harmonizes with the color of the iris. The latter gives name to the color of the eye. The iris is a band which surrounds the hole or pupil. It is through this opening the light travels to the brain, exciting the optic nerve and receiving interpretation at the end of the journey.

The color of the eyes is determined by the band: if this is brown the eyes are brown. The pupil of the eye is not supposed to have color; it is really a dark hole, and no color can be seen in a dark hole.

The pupil of the eye denotes the magnetic condition. When there is little energy the pupil is exceedingly small, unless the person is subject to abnormal nervous conditions. The reason for the pupil being small is due to the lack of vitality in the optic nerve and brain. Blue eyes have a large field of blue when the pupils are contracted. The same is true of gray eyes, or in fact any color, but as the magnetic forces become active, the field becomes smaller because the pupil of the eye expands, and the aperture becomes enlarged to the extent of the energy within taking possession of the orb. Under great nervous excitement the pupil, black, blazing and intense, causes this curtain to open so wide that there is no trace of the iris, and consequently no color to the eye.

An orator's eyes which are deep blue, when addressing an audience in an eloquent manner, will change to black. The gray eyes of an actor under great excitement will turn black for the evening. This is a very common occurrence, although it may not be noticed as often as it really occurs.

Those who are able to master the will of others have consciously or unconsciously been able to expand the pupil of their eye. The person realizes that a change is taking place in the one before him, but does not understand what it is. He may be influenced in this way in a wonderful degree, yet he has not been put into a hypnotic sleep.

The eyes of the most magnetic men, when they are alone, become as though they were dead—the fire slumbers, but has not gone out. When they wish to increase their magnetism the pupil becomes enlarged. They need not use the power all the time, therefore it is not aroused. Real magnetic men and women do not permit this power to manifest itself, except when they want to use it; at other times they may appear the very opposite to what they really are and their eyes will appear apparently lifeless and will often even drop li_e those in a sleep. Most of the time they are really only resting their forces, thus being better prepared when it is necessary for them to put forward extra energy.

Personal magnetism regulates the normal expansion of the pupil and it may be controlled at will. Thought is the offspring of will, and may be put into execution, so magnetism may be aroused in the same way, or, on the other hand, it may remain dormant as much or as little as its possessor pleases. As this is a fact, it must follow that a magnetic person may expand or contract the pupil at will.

"An expanded eye-pupil exerts an influence over a beholder."

Animals make use of the expansion. By this means they are able to secure their prey. The cat, for instance, illustrates this. A strong light will contract the pupil of the eye; darkness expands it. These changes are of importance. However, a cat can, by willing, reverse these conditions. For example: a cat may be standing in the full glare of the sun with the iris completely covering the pupil, then can reverse this condition upon seeing a bird, although the sun naturally closes up the pupil, the energy of the will within can open it to its widest extent, for if this were not so, the animal would possess no power over its prey.

It is a well known fact that the conscious insensibility to pain which accompanies the capture of a human being by a wild animal is caused by something in the expanded pupils and glaring balls of the captor, which has lessened the will of the prey, and the sensation of drowsyness which follows may deaden the feeling in the nerves. There are many autheticated cases of freedom from pain while in the clutches of a savage beast, the hunter saying: ''I was quite conscious of the tiger's teeth penetrating my shoulder, yet, instead of its hurting me, I felt no pain whatever.

No human being possesses the power of standing calmly before the gaze of one who is able to expand the pupils of the eye under magnetic energy without being affected. One of the two following results must take place:

The person is either made drowsy by the hypnotic tendency, or the person is aroused to admiration.

This is natural force, and is very common. It is a well known fact that a man can hold a wild animal at bay by a steadfast gaze, though few would be willing to take the chances of so frail a defense. The defense, however, would be sufficient so long as the man would be able to maintain the energy of power of the eye. If the animal magnetism of the beast be of a stronger quality, the vitality of the man will be broken. This the beasts nave learned to expect, drowsiness follows. and soon all is over. But we have many verified cases of men who have withstood the gaze of savage beasts and have actually cowed them by their eyes.

You have, no doubt, visited a zoo, and have noticed how the keeper, by the use of his eyes, has controlled refractory beasts that chafe in captivity. The eye of the keeper reduces the spirit of the animal. There is a low growl, a muttering of malice, a crouching to spring; the animal's eyes are charged with energy, his pupil becomes expanded and drives out all the solar from the iris. The keeper is in the cage, and he knows that if he can not control the animal by his eyes he would be devoured. He knows, should he turn his eyes away, it would be all over with him. This will give you some idea as to the importance of the eyes.

Have you not at times, in some unexpected and unexplained manner, given your consent to certain things, when it was really contrary to your better judgment? In other words, we know that at such times we have been controlled by others.

Some day we will learn more about how we lose control, and yield. Very often in the beginning we are quite positive we will not yield, but shortly after a change takes place, and we believe it's the right thing to do.

One of our most successful men, when asked what his opinion was of the many failures of men who start a promising life, said: "Of all the facts that operate to make our lives doubtful in their success or failure, the most important is the appalling ease with which, on some unforseen occasion, and in some unexpected manner, we yield advantages which our better judgment should have clung to and held in its keeping." In other words, we are not always able to take care of ourselves.

Mental Power of Control.

The searcher after truth has now begun to realize that there are mighty powers of nature that are ready to be developed.

Those who wish, can reach and control others. We are now ready to develop a Higher Power than we have ever possessed, but this higher power must be used for the good of humanity. If used for any other purpose, it will soon perish.

If **you** will carefully study the **following** instructions you will be able to accomplish feats which you perhaps now think are impossible.

"Man's Powers are Actually Miraculous and Measureless."

Think this over carefully!

"Thought" is now recognized as the ruling force of the Universe. Everything that takes place is the result of the Human Will, supplemented by Human Thought.

It is now admitted by the medical profession that mental suggestion will nulify the effects of a great many medicines. Also, the flow of blood has often been stopped through power of will. If man is able to control the forces of the human body, does it not sound reasonable that he can control the forces of nature outside the body?

The secret of gaining control over others, **and to** be able to read their minds, is to be able to place yourself in sympathy with **them.** When you do **this** it creates a soul-influence which can be cultivated and can be **made to** manifest and exerted to a wonderful **degree** for your own benefit and that of **others.**

By using our will we are able to transfer **our** thoughts to others to take the place of those which they previously had. The magnetic ether can be used by the will, either by its conscious or subconscious action, to dominate the other person's actions. When we are to control his mind, we can also control his body, as this is under the control of the mind.

When you begin to realize the possibilities of mind control, you will have a joyous, happy feeling. It gives you strength and decision of character.

In order to acquire the ability to manage and control others in social and business dealings, it is necessary for you to be in good health. The Magnetic Ether used by the Will is generated in the nerve centers of the body, and rapidly passes through the body. This is found in the largest quantities in people who are in the best of health, and least in those whose system is nearly exhausted.

Therefore, if you wish to learn to influence others, you must give the necessary attention to perfecting the physical body. This is not difficult, as there are a great many excellent books on the subject.

Few people realize what a wonderful part physical health plays in their success. Without good health we cannot have a strong, active brain.

When the body is weak, the brain power will become affected, as the Magnetic Ether is developed in the nerve centers of the body. When the body is lacking in vitality, it cannot generate as much of the Magnetic Ether as it would if it were strong.

The person with weak nerve-force becomes sensitive and weak in confidence and Will Power. If you do not have confidence in yourself, you will not be able to exert the proper amount of will power to transfer your thoughts to the minds of others. The will regulates the amount of Ether expended, and is the propelling force. The will sets all the forces of the brain and body to work, and directs their actions.

In starting your practices it is well to start with small things first, and gradually increase the tests until you are able to accomplish greater things. Confidence and perseverance is all that is necessary. Confidence comes with success. With each success our confidence and ability increases, and harder tests can be undertaken with still greater confidence. The person without confidence loses his own individuality and is controlled by others, being afraid to try his own influence upon others.

The Art and Science of Controlling People Without Their Knowledge.

The greatest orators are those of intense magnetic force. They not only realize that they possess it, but know how to use it. They use it to attract and keep the attention of the audience they are addressing. They use the subtle nerve-force to influence and control the minds of their hearers, so as to gain their attention to the magnetic words they are speaking. All great orators possess the power of concentration. Before they deliver a message they first study it over carefully and deliver it to their subjective mind in their own study. During that time they think of nothing but this subject, shutting out all other thought. This is what every one should do before proceeding with any great performance.

It is said that, when Patrick Henry was a young man, he spent his leisure in fishing in a small mountain stream near by his home, where he would sit for hours rarely bringing home any fish. On one occasion some one saw him seemingly watching his cork from which the fish had long since devoured the bait. He would watch the crow for hours, paying absolutely no attention to anything that was going on around him. He used this means to develop concentration. If you want to develop Personal Magnetism in its fullest extent, you must develop concentration, which must precede any great undertaking. Concentration of thought strengthens the mind and places it in a receptive condition to receive thoughts and suggestions from the subjective mind from which we can receive superior information.

You understand then why it is very important for you to learn to concentrate your thoughts on one thing at a time. You can thus receive the information it is important for you to know. The person who is able to concentrate can, when necessary, be in a positive state, which is needed in order to send forth the thoughts with the power needed to control others.

I was asked by one of my students a short time ago if it were not wrong to place one's self in the negative state. Should one not always be positive? There are two kinds of electricity, as all scientists acknowledge: the positive and the negative electricity. The first has a maximum of intensity, but a minimum of quality, while the latter possesses the greatest quantity but the least intensity. Now in the "positive" state we use the flash referred to previously; the "negative" state being just the opposite.

If, therefore, you wish to influence a single person (or a number of them) to think or act the way you wish them to, you must surcharge yourself with a quantity of magnetic force. In order to do this you must previously devote sufficient time to concentration on the subject so as to be filled with it from head to foot. When you are in this state magnetic force will fairly stream from your eyes as a positive force into the eyes of the other person, or audience, you may wish to influence. They will be impressed with your earnestness and sincerity and will give you their closest attention. As you speak your magnetic force will thrill their subjective minds with justice and truthfulness of every word you utter, and they will believe what you say to be true. You will notice also that all magnetic orators will use their hands in a calm, deliberate way, as if they were believing what they are stating. This belief gives

them a certain power which transforms their
enthusiasm to their hearers, for, while an
orator is pointing his forefinger at his audience, magnetism is flowing from his finger-
tips, which helps him drive home the thoughts
with a sledge-hammer force. A speaker uses
his greatest personal magnetism when he
clinches an unanswerable argument. It is
then he uses the strongest mental suggestion.

Any man who can mentally suggest his
thoughts to the subjective minds of others is
bound to become a leader among men. Ideas
thus implanted take root, and bear fruit in
time.

It has been said that unless a person is
honest, earnest, sincere and absolutely truthful he cannot develop Personal Magnetism.
From my experience I would say that this is
nearly true. You may develop Personal Magnetism to a limited extent without the possession of all these, but the more you have of
the qualifications, the more highly you will
develop it.

In order to exert the greatest amount of attractive influence on those you come in contact with, we must make it a point to think
the same thoughts of them which we would

have them think of us. Not only must you *pretend* to think as you act, but you must really do so. If you wish to have power over people in general, your thoughts must be of a pure and elevating nature. If we think thoughts of kindness, we are sure to reap a rich harvest for "whatsoever a man soweth, that shall he reap." "Like begets like"— the world over. A smile begets a smile; kind thoughts produce kind thoughts in others. If we live a life of love and kindness, those with whom we associate will feel the attraction of our loving and kindly thoughts, and, as a consequence, will be attracted towards us, and thus be helpful.

This is a valuable secret in the study of Personal Magnetism. There may be some who think it wrong to control others, but we must have a leader who possesses self-confidence without egotism.

When we wish to control others we exercise the positive functions of our mind to impose the force upon others, so that they may do our bidding.

When we exercise the negative or attracting quality, we draw the respect and regard and love of others to ourselves. The positive then, you will understand, is valuable in controlling, while the negative is used to attract.

We should let no one come into our presence without using our influence trying to dominate him. I know of a man who developed himself in a very short time from a clerk in a store to the manager of a large business, just by this practice. When he would meet a man, no matter who it might be, he would say to himself, "I can dominate you; my will power is stronger than yours." There was such a sudden change in him that people were puzzled and thought at first that he was out of his head. He made the mistake of talking too much about what he was going to do. I would advise you to keep your own counsel, and watch results. But do not think it is wrong to control others, as, consciously or unconsciously, when two people meet, one or the other dominates; as Emerson says: "He who has more soul than I, rules me." When you control others you are the one who has the most soul. If the person is not passive to your influence, you must use your power to make him passive; you must send thoughts to him which will dominate his mind, and crowd out all his own active or positive thoughts in the following manner.

"You will do as I say; you will yield." "I will control you; I am your Master." Think such thoughts as these for the moment, and what you want him to do or tell us you must either mentally or verbally speak to him in a positive, forceful and enthusiastic way, being confident that you will rule and dominate his actions. Be firm, do not yield. Do not hold a single doubt as to your success. No matter what conditions may arise which you had not contemplated, do not falter or be lacking in power. Exclude every thought from your mind but the one thought which you wish to impress upon the other person. Concentrate on this and be confident that you will influence the person, and you surely will. Thought is creative power. It is a force and can accomplish with unerring certainty whatever mission we commit to its care—if we never change our mind and recall it.

The second exercise is one which I consider very valuable, as it has a very far-reaching effect. Select some one whom you dislike, and who has shown that he dislikes you. Both positive and negative qualities must be used. Make it a point to meet this person face to face, and, if possible, engage him in conversation, saying emphatically to yourself: "I command that this person shall **feel my influence**. I will that this person change his opinion of me, and be attracted towards **me**, and to feel my influence continually. **I will** that this good impression I have made **shall** not be shaken off." Also think such **thoughts** as these: "From now on you will like **me**; you will be my friend." Your thoughts, **so** expressed, will find lodgment in the person's mind. Impressions made in this **manner** upon the consciousness of another person **are** some times indelible. In this way **you can** mould the opinions of other people into **obedi**ence to your will, and they will be **attracted** towards you, and will feel no resentment.

For the third illustration, let us **suppose** that we wish to influence some one at a distance. Say to yourself: "I command **this** person to feel my influence. I will this **person** to sit down and write me a letter." **If you** have developed your mind and will-power **as** taught in the *"Master Mind," your command will be obeyed. However, you must be confident that you will succeed. After a few tests you will be convinced of the interchange of messages. There are many different **ways** to experiment. For instance, if you are interested in finding out something about the character of another, you can send him such thoughts as will make him reveal his true nature to you. Say, for instance: "I want you to show me what you really are."

Or, for example, you can select some one whom you wish to help you in a business way. While he is in your presence hold the thought: "You have a good opinion of me; you think I have the making of a good business man. You will help me along all you can because you have confidence in me." Just concentrate your mind a moment on some particular thing you wish this person to do for you, then proceed with the matters that need your attention. A little practice will convince you that there are powers you never dreamed of that can be used to bring you success. When you use these forces constantly you develop a wonderful power, and become master of the situation, no matter what it is. In a short time you will be able to involuntarily, unconsciously, and without effort, control others because you will have developed more will power. The mental forces, as is the case with the muscles of the arm, increase with use.

Never be in a hurry with your experiments. Haste very often delays the developments desired. You cannot expect to jump with one leap from the bottom of the ladder to the top. Many a failure has been caused by not taking time for the necessary preparation, which is a sign of weakness and lack of self control. The secret of sure, ultimate success is to proceed in a calm, deliberate manner, determined to master each step.

Control yourself and you can control those with whom you come in contact. In your daily transactions preserve a calm demeaner. Start everything you undertake with a firm consciousness that you are using but a small part of your force—that you still have plenty of reserve force which you can call upon in case it is necessary.

Try to avoid nervous, jerky movements and mannerisms. Make a study of yourself. See how many unnecessary movements you make. Let your motions be easy, rather than sharp. The quick jerk of the hand or arm throws off magnetism, just like it would throw off water if it were wet.

There is one thing I wish to caution you about. Do not let your mind dwell on the impressions which you are making on others.

Keep your own counsel, as I have said above, and practice your experiments persistently, believing in yourself thoroughly. You have within you all the latent power that is necessary to make you a very magnetic man or woman.

Whenever you attend a lecture or a theatre, or mingle with people of culture and refinement, study them. You should aim to perfect your manners, and suppress the element of vanity. Never speak of yourself unless conversation almost actually forces you to do so—and then let the subject drop as soon as possible. Be interested, however, in what others have to say of themselves. Encourage them to speak of their experiences, as you will thus be likely to receive many valuable pointers. When you begin to realize your latent power, you need no flattery. To seek others' opinion of you is a weakness. When you learn not to overestimate the value of the approval of others, you will then receive it lavishly. This rule is a rule that every one of great knowledge and power knows to be true.

The silent man is usually the man of force. He never tells his secrets or talks of his knowledge. "Great men are reserved in manner." They talk little; they are self reliant. They stand firmly on their own feet. They do not need a prop, or have to lean on others. It is only the weak who are ever giving and receiving confidences. They tell all they know. "The shallow brook proclaims its presence loudly; but the deep river is silent in its flow." By reserving your knowledge you increase your capacity to receive, and preserve that which you already have.

You must be enthusiastic, or else you will not have courage to tackle the big things in life. Realizing the importance of certain undertakings spurs you on to accomplish-them. Be positive in thought and action, asserting your thoughts with the air of positive conviction if you wish to carry the fullest influence of your speech. You must have a positive attitude of the mind when you wish to exert a great influence over others. This cannot be emphasized too strongly. The two master forces are Thought and Will. We use them to become masters in every sphere of life. Never let a little opposition alter your course. When obstacles try to interfere with you, put forward a greater force, use tact and good judgment, and you can overwhelm your adversaries. To make up your mind to do

something is half the battle. If you entertain doubt, he will be your guest. Whatever
you think, there is a possibility to it. Courage
brings victory; timidity defeat. He with the
strong will masters fate, instead of being a
victim of circumstances.

"The Mind in the Man and the Will in the
Man's Executive Mind is the Master, and the
Body is the Servant to the Mind."

Every day you are consciously or unconsciously moulding your character by your
actions and habits. You are a result of good
or evil influences.

There are three channels by which we can
use personal magnetism and can direct its
flow through any one, or all, at the command
of our will. These outlets are the voice, the
eyes and the hands. It has always been an
open question as to which is the strongest
channel, as they differ in different people.
The eyes and the voice are used most. The
person who is able to use the three simul-
taneously is the strongest. When all three
are combined, the ether projected by the will
produces an influence so strong that it can
dominate the mind of almost any person.

Before you attempt to use your power, you
should first decide what you wish to accom-

plish. You should decide on an object at the time, and keep this in your mind, and direct all your energies to the accomplishment of that purpose. Do not let that object slip from your mind for an instant. By your will power you must direct your thoughts to pass, with the ether, through your eyes, your voice and your hands.

When you use your eyes, gaze at the person you intend to influence, focusing your sight between his eyes or at the root of his nose. When using the voice, speak clearly, and with feeling; use a moderate tone and never speak too loudly or spasmodically—but you ought to lower your voice a trifle. Your subject will then have to concentrate his mind in order to hear what you say. This you will realize to be a very valuable point. Do not let your voice tremble, as this denotes a lack of self-confidence, and this would destroy the good impression you may have made.

When you wish to use the hands to impart magnetism, be sure to shake hands with the person. Put plenty of life in the handshake, taking a firm grip of the whole hand—but never press it too hard. Give the hand two firm shakes, and hold it for a second—then let go of it quickly. You must hold the thought that you wish to impress the person favorably with your force. Do not, however, make the mistake of holding the hand for over a second, for if you do, the subject will feel the influence so strongly that he may become aware of a feeling that you are trying to influence him, and may intuitively read your thoughts and your intentions. This of course you do not want him to do.

The hands can also be used to good advantage without even touching the person. Stand or sit within five or six feet from the subject and have your right hand rest so that the fingers will be pointing in the direction of him. Then will that your wishes shall be passed through that hand to the person's mind. This method, when used in conjunction with the voice and the eye can be made very effective.

You must also remember that you are likely to be influenced by the Magnetic Ether of other people, if you are not on your guard. Just remember that the positive and strong mind rejects the influences which come to it. The negative, or weak, will accepts the influences and thoughts of others and thinks they are his own. Your self protection depends on keeping your will power positive.

The strong man is the one who dictates to others through his thoughts. Again I warn you, let your intentions always be good. Evil thoughts not only affect yourself, but those around you.

After you have become powerful, you will unconsciously influence those around you. For this reason you must be careful of what you think. Always keep in mind: he who can master himself, has no difficulty in mastering others.

How to Influence Different Kinds of People.

There are no two persons just alike in the world, therefore we cannot influence any two by the same method and get the best results. I will classify the people with whom you are most likely to come in contact.

Naturally, in order to influence any one you must first know who it is, and in order to secure the greatest success you must know something of his strong and weak points. If you have never seen him before, but have studied Professor Dumont's "Character Analysis From Features of Head and Face," you will be able to judge him pretty well.

From the features you can determine a person's strong and weak points, etc.

The person with magnetism has the power to influence any one to a greater or less degree, but if you do not know the subject's natural tendencies, it will be harder for you to make him think and act as you wish. If you attempt to use the same means with every one, you will fail nine times out of ten, and naturally you will give up the whole matter quickly. The reason so many fail to exert their influence over others is that they do not use the right method.

Every one has weaknesses, but they do not like to be told of them. Therefore, you will have to be careful, and not antagonize a person by referring to his hobbies or weaknesses. Instead, cater to his idiosyncrasies; pretend they are yours also, and this will flatter him. Remember to always keep the objects you wish to attain foremost in your mind, and constantly will that the person shall do exactly as you wish. When you shake a man's hand, and there is something you wish him to do, clasp his hand warmly, look him straight in the eye, and at the same time will what you wish him to do. If you will just exert your will-power and feel confident of success, you will be able to exert a wonderful influence over the person. It is easy to make friends with some people. Others are slower to respond, and it takes longer to make your influence felt enough to gain their favor. But never become discouraged, though you may not succeed at first. It is a well known fact that the constant dripping of water will wear away the hardest stone, so it is with personal magnetism. You are bound to succeed if you do not become discouraged.

First Example.

The most difficult person to influence is the one of a strong, domineering Will-Power. You must possess a great deal of aggressive force to influence him, otherwise you would be very likely to fail. Therefore, in order to succeed, you must use tact. You must approach him by a different method, and first gain his friendship and sympathy. You can appear to be humble, and pretend to admire his excellent qualities, ignoring his weaknesses. If you will praise him, he will believe in you. He cannot see his own faults, nor must you. If you will raise him on a pinnacle far above yourself, you will both merit and receive his favor. So long as you show appreciation of him, you can get him to do almost anything you wish him to do. The following true story will show how the most difficult subject may be influenced.

An old man, at the head of a large wholesale drug company was of the uncivil, rough, domineering type. When a salesman called on him he would treat him as if he were going to devour him. However, a man of this kind is as easy to handle as any other, if you walk into his office, make your statements clear and forceful, look him straight in the eye, and not let him think for a moment that there is any doubt but that you have something of vital interest to him. The mistake, however, must not be made of appealing to his good judgment, as this would make him stop and think, thus probably defeating your plans. It matters not who the man is, he respects the qualities of force, energy and confidence. No one admires weakness.

Those who have the stronger will, always will be the dictators. Hence, if you develop a strong magnetic will, you will become a master and dominate others' thoughts as well as their actions. What we then will them to do, they will do.

It is very often found that people who are deficient in will-power possess a certain stubborness, which is some times taken for will-power. However, there is a big difference between the two. Never force your ideas or opinions upon those of this class, never display any unruliness, because this would quickly make them obstinate. You can very quickly and easily tell a stubborn person; he is not the one with a strong will, therefore you can make him obey your orders, if you will use but tact in giving them. The stubborn person does not like to take orders, but by saying to him "don't you think so and so is all right," etc., etc., he can usually be made to think as you would have him. If not, then it is generally best not to say any more at that time, but await a better opportunity, and figure out a different plan, alway; however, acting as if seeking his judgment. The facts are: you suggest the ideas, and he speaks them. Think this over, and you will realize the importance. Never forget the important part of keeping your eyes on him, and your desires firmly in your mind.

Second Example.

If the person is intuitive (and our race at

present is more or less so), you can accomplish your purpose without saying a word to him, by concentrating your mind upon him, and willing that he carry out your wishes—always thinking of what you wish him to do. Your desires are communicated to him telepathically, and he receives them and thinks they are his own. This is a very successful way of influencing people. If possible, sit behind the person, so that your eyes do not meet his, and look at the base of his brain while sending him your wishes. This is what is known as wireless mental telegraphy. Many have successfully tried this test. They see some one at a gathering in front of them, and wish that person to recognize them. They concentrate their mind on him for a few minutes, the person feels the inclination to turn around, which he finally does and looks at them. It is really wonderful what a person with a strong will can accomplish. If you will confidently and calmly will some one to obey your orders, he will do so.

Third Example.

Say the next person you wish to influence has a very violent temper. In that case you must talk quietly to him, never letting yourself get excited and using a well modulated, smooth tone of voice. This will have a quieting effect on the nerves and temper of the person to be influenced. "Temper is uncontrolled emotion"; therefore, you must not do anything to arouse the feelings of this person. You must aim to produce a soothing, quieting effect upon his nerves; it is a waste of time to try to influence a person until he is in a calm mood. He cannot think intelligently until he is. If you will conduct yourself properly he will soon calm down, no matter how much he may have lost control over his emotions. Keep your object the most prominent thing in your mind, and he will think the same as you do. The person who quickly loses his temper, reason and will-power, is not properly balanced. If you can just get him to cool down, you will have little trouble in getting him to accede to your wishes. Never, however, try to argue with him when he has lost control of his temper. It is far better to leave him for the present. The next time you meet him he will be different. By remaining calm your remarks will have made an impression, and when quieted down, he will, more or less, unconsciously meditate

upon your remarks and will be better prepared to entertain your proposition the next
time you see him. It will then be easy for
you to accomplish your purpose. It is a great
help to learn not to lose control of your feelings, or to arouse the feelings of others. The
person with deficient will-power must eventually yield to the person of strong will-power.
If you would attempt to argue with a person
who is not in a normal condition, and try to
force him to accept your views as correct, it
would be very hard for you to secure his attention again, as you would have aroused the
antagonism of his entire nature against you,
and any statement you might make, he would
vigorously oppose.

Fourth Example.

Those who can be most readily influenced
are the ones who are continually putting
things off. They are very flexible, and you
can quickly make them think the way you
want them to. You must secure their decided
answer at the time however, or, by tomorrow,
some one else may have completely changed
their decisions. You cannot depend on the
impression you have made when the person

is out of your presence, you can only control him absolutely while he is with you. Generally such persons are cowardly, and are continually afraid they will make a mistake, and in order to avoid this they will tell a lie if this will get them out of it. They are like a machine: they need proper motive power to make them useful. For the time being you must become their engineer, and direct their thoughts and actions, which is easy to do if you can secure their confidence and appeal to their sympathies. They can be ruled by their hearts instead of their heads, and therefore, you can quickly learn how to appeal to them. They will often do what you wish, just for fear they will cause you trouble, or appear ungrateful.

Fifth Example.

If the person you wish to influence has extravagant ideas as to the use of money, you can get from him anything you wish. Just keep your eyes fixed on his, and assume a friendly air, and he will do what you want him to do.

Sixth Example.

If the person be nervous, critical and skeptical, he will have an exalted opinion of his own ideas, and can only see flaws in others. This is a very difficult person to influence, and it will be necessary for you to use all the diplomacy and tact you possess to influence him. The first thing you must do is to quiet his nerves (which can be done by directing your mind and thoughts to this purpose). Avoid criticising his actions and statements, even though they may be wrong. If you oppose him, he will become irritable, and in this state you would be wasting time trying to influence him. As I said before, he is a hard case, but do not become discouraged. You will have to make several attempts before you will accomplish your purpose, but perseverance will win out finally. Never give up. Lay your plans carefully, and eliminate every possible flaw. Don't become discouraged if he criticises and tears to pieces every one of your plans. It is very likely he will suggest a number of changes, but if you can only agree with him, you can gradually bring him to see that your ideas are his—though giving him credit, and you will thus be able to influence him to do as you wish.

Seventh Example.

In dealing with the very practical person, you must be careful about any statements you make. They must appear truthful, practical, intelligent and logical. Never over-exaggerate. Look him straight in the eyes with a frank, honest expression. Keep your gaze steadfastly fixed upon him. Usually he is a pretty good judge of human nature. If you look in any other direction while talking to him he will lose confidence in you. This is very important; do not forget it. You must gain his confidence if you are to be successful. He can be depended on to deal squarely and honestly with you. That which he promises he will carry out. He will keep his promises in the manner stipulated. Never try to flatter him directly, but you can influence him by showing by your actions that you value his judgment and opinion. Your statements and requests should be clear and to the point. Speak in a quiet, but firm voice, and never make any statements that you cannot prove. He does not want you to waste his time with words. He wants you to state your business in as few words as possible—and then stop and give him a chance to think your statements over and decide their value. Unless your proposition is one of merit, you will waste your time talking to him.

Eighth Example.

If you have a plan that is original, and you need some backing to float it, select some one who you know is able to do it. A man of independence. Such a man's finger will be broad and flat, like a painter's brush. A man with this characteristic is energetic and loves action. In order to influence him you must be very enthusiastic and emotional, rather than logical, but you must state your proposition quickly. He is continually on the lookout for something new; he likes to tackle new schemes. He likes to give way to his feelings, rather than his judgment. Such a man will make many errors, but he works and makes the successes pay for the failures. He needs a good deal of talking to before you can convince him. Get him to talk also. You must, however, have some definite plan arranged to place before him, otherwise he will be likely to become interested in some other scheme, for he is generally interested in the scheme which is freshest in his mind. You must keep him enthused, and as long as you do he will work night and day for the success of your plan. But be sure and keep your desire prominently in your mind, and be with his as much as possible, so that you will be able to telepathically convey your ideas to him, and he will think they are his own.

Ninth Example.

Then there are those who are known as the _norbid and melancholy set. It seems that it is their very nature to be sad. They think circumstances are against them; nothing appears bright and cheerful, and they believe gayety and frivolity to be immoral. With these people you must pretend to be as they are. They think luck has been against them. They like to hear of hard experiences, and you can gain their attention if you will show a depth of sadness in your voice, and sorrow in your eyes. The more you can show your sympathy with them, the more they will sympathize with you. When you reach this point you will have little difficulty receiving from them what you wish.

Tenth Example.

In dealing with a person who is very systematic, you must also show that you believe in system and method. You must be careful in your appearance, speech and deportment. He will notice all these. If you are neat in appearance, spotlessly clean, bear a well-possessed manner and walk and talk with an air of firmness and a full supply of nerve-force, you will be sure to make a good impression and he will pay especial attention to your statements.

Eleventh Example.

Then there is just the opposite class to those explained above—those who pay practically no attention to detail. They are careless in appearance, and have a natural dislike for system. They see the affair as a whole, and do not think it worth while to pay attention to the little details. In dealing with this class, it will not be necessary to pay any special attention to your dress. If you appear to them too well groomed they will be likely to size you up as being too "finicky" and "foppish" and think that you

waste too much of your time on your appearance and not enough on the real and substan-
tial things of life. In dealing with this class
you must come to the point at once. Make
your statements in a clear manner and do
not use any unnecessary words. It is well
to speak as rapidly as you can, that is to
say, not in a fast manner, but coming to the
point quickly, because no matter how quickly
you state your plan, he will have intuitively
"sensed" your statement before you have
finished talking. This class is naturally very
intuitive, and if you keep your eyes on theirs
and your plans in your mind constantly
while speaking, they will be ready to give you
a definite answer by the time you are through.

Twelfth Example.

The person of the material instinct can be
reached better through material things.
Usually he is a lover of good eating, and the
quickest way to reach him is through his
stomach. Invite him to the best dinner you
can buy, and show him that you are used to
the best things. You will quickly secure his
O. K., and he will show you that he is even
more generous than you are. This is the time

to bring forth your plans. It will not be wise to state in plain words what you want and ask his help, but rather, in a sort of confidential way, show him your plans and remark that you are going to look for some one who is in a position to do so and so. He will not be likely to say anything at the time, but your suggestions will have made an impression and it will take root and germinate. Then some time when you least expect it, he will show his interest and grant your wishes. This is the way he likes to do things. You must seem surprised and be generous in your expressions of thanks and appreciation of his courtesy. He will then be quite willing to grant you any favor you might wish.

Thirteenth Example.

It is really remarkable how the student of human nature can judge a person by merely shaking hands. When you shake a man's hand that is limp, you will find that he is lazy and selfish at heart. He can be very easily influenced, but he will either grant your wishes at once, or not at all. He may seem very friendly, and promise all you ask, but as

soon as you are out of his sight you will be
forgotten, and you will lose your influence
over him until you see him again—when he
will have plenty of excuses to offer why he
failed to keep his promise. If you will carefully study any of the excuses he gives, you
will find that they are not logical. He cannot
be depended upon when he is out of your
sight; it is really not worth while wasting
time on such a person, if it can be avoided.
You will find the same rule applying to those
people who merely place the tips of their fingers in your hand, and make little or no response to your grasp. These people are
heartless and selfish, and care only for their
own interests. The time spent on them is
usually wasted. The magnetic man feels like
throwing the hand of such a person away the
moment he touches it, as there comes over
him a feeling of repulsion, and a desire to
have nothing more to do with them.

Fourteenth Example.

If you wish to influence persons of the opposite sex, never be too demonstrative. It
is the rule of human nature to desire what
is kept from it, or what cannot be gotten.

That which is obtained without a struggle is esteemed of little value. You may be courteous, kind and affectionate, but you must not express your love until you feel that you have won the object of your desire.

Owing to you possessing animal and personal magnetism it is comparatively easy to influence the opposite sex. If you will wisely use these two you will seldom fail, providing you are honest and sincere in your attentions. Your success will depend upon the amount of personal magnetism you have developed, and the degree of control you have over yourself. The more personal magnetism you develop, the stronger both mentally and physically you will become.

If you will study Professor Dumont's "Personal Success Series," and follow the instructions given therein, you will fit yourself for the very best position in the land, and make your life a permanent success. The rules found in this series have been followed by all successful people. It is very often they follow them intuitively, not really conscious of doing so. The chances are they do not really know what caused them to climb the ladder of success. Their friends call them "lucky," but it was not luck. They used their personal magnetism, which all possess to a greater or less degree. Those who do not develop and use this power, will not gain any great success. Personal magnetism is the key to the innermost secrets of human nature. Those who have studied the examples given in the foregoing will be able to discover the weak and strong points in the character of every one they come in contact with, and know how to attack their weakest points. This is of the greatest advantage.

The great secret of all personal influence is to make the other party admire your judgment. The best way to do this is to praise his judgment. The great majority of the human race possess sufficient vanity to induce them to believe us when we pretend to believe in them. Sympathize with the plans of others, and be a good listener to all they may have to say. It is remarkable what an effect this little action has on every one. It is natural for people to like those who favor their opinions. They will cultivate their society, and think their judgment good, and thus be easily influenced by their suggestions.

A Final Word.

By just merely reading over this course

you cannot expect to acquire **very** much power, nor will you thereby know whether the claims made are true. However, every one who will make a thorough study of the lessons can really attain the influence **over** others that he desires.

Those who know me personally, **know that** I would not make a statement I did not believe to be true. I will ask you **to study** these lessons faithfully. Do not have **a single** doubt in your mind, but believe that you can do anything that is stated, and I know **that** you will develop the wonderful power of controlling the actions of others and make **them** think as you direct. **You** will secure the best results if you will **read** only one lesson **a** day, and then study and ponder over it **again** and again until you thoroughly understand it and are able to write out from memory **the** different rules given. They will help **you to** rise to the pinnacle of success in your **chosen** field, without **depending** on Miss Elusive Chance. If you do not rise to a position of eminence in this world, it is your own **fault**.

We are now entering a psychic age. **We** **will** not only be able to do all that we **think** **we** can do, but also things which **we, at** **present**, cannot conceive. After once **master-**

ing the science of Personal Magnetism, you can use it to gain wonderful Psychic Power. All the forces of the universe can ultimately be controled by you. All the physical, mental and spiritual forces are at your disposal to be used for the good.

It has been my intention to make this work as practical as possible, and I know that a great many will find it so. Remember, however, that a great attainment was never accomplished in a day. Development comes from study growth. This is especially true of the mental forces. It is "line after line, and precept upon precept," that finally gives you development. Start in today and devote a small part of each evening reading Professor Dumont's Personal Success Series, and from this day on you will develop all your latent power that now is dormant.

Au revoir, my magnetic friends. We shall meet again, in due time.

Finis.

COSIMO CLASSICS

COSIMO is an innovative publisher of books and publications that inspire, inform and engage readers worldwide. Our titles are drawn from a range of subjects including health, business, philosophy, history, science and sacred texts. We specialize in using print-on-demand technology (POD), making it possible to publish books for both general and specialized audiences and to keep books in print indefinitely. With POD technology new titles can reach their audiences faster and more efficiently than with traditional publishing.

> ➤ **Permanent Availability:** Our books & publications never go out-of-print.

> ➤ **Global Availability:** Our books are always available online at popular retailers and can be ordered from your favorite local bookstore.

COSIMO CLASSICS brings to life unique, rare, out-of-print classics representing subjects as diverse as *Alternative Health, Business and Economics, Eastern Philosophy, Personal Growth, Mythology, Philosophy, Sacred Texts, Science, Spirituality* and much more!

COSIMO-on-DEMAND publishes your books, publications and reports. If you are an Author, part of an Organization, or a Benefactor with a publishing project and would like to bring books back into print, publish new books fast and effectively, would like your publications, books, training guides, and conference reports to be made available to your members and wider audiences around the world, we can assist you with your publishing needs.

Visit our website at www.cosimobooks.com to learn more about Cosimo, browse our catalog, take part in surveys or campaigns, and sign-up for our newsletter.

And if you wish please drop us a line at info@cosimobooks.com. We look forward to hearing from you.

CPSIA information can be obtained
at www.ICGtesting.com
Printed in the USA
BVHW072252170322
631650BV00004B/455